# THE ROAD TO

# HANCOCK

## COUNTY

## FROM TRAGEDY TO TRIUMPH

# JAMES ODELL

ISBN: 979-8-218-07816-4

# FOREWORD

As of this writing Mississippi is the most incarcerated state in the most incarcerated nation in the "world". Mississippi is also the poorest of the fifty states in the United States of America with the lowest per capita income per year, and Mississippi ranks forty-ninth in education of the fifty states.

But Mississippi is also a national leader in the category of residents who claim belief in God and is near the top of those who pray daily. Ironically, church attendance per capita is among the lowest in the nation. Life is complex, isn't it?

Interestingly, it would be the State of Mississippi where author James O'Dell would be incarcerated and write the story of his life and his transformation. In *The Road to Hancock County*, Jay traces his life from conman to convert and organized crime syndicate member to inspirational religious leader within the inmate population where he has been incarcerated since 2018.

As you read this book consider that James O'Dell grew to adulthood, without a formal education and was largely raised in boy's homes and the criminal justice system. Texas would be the state in which he grew to maturity, and the one where he reached the lowest points in his life.

Gifted with a superb intellect, James would go on to use the skills of organization and manipulation of those with power and money to amass several small fortunes, only to squander each of them. He would spend his teenage years and his adult life into his late thirties chasing money, women and chemical intoxication to the point of moral and physical destruction.

Finally it would be the love of God which would chase James down and in a holding cell in the Hancock County Jail in South Mississippi, begin a transformation which would take him from tragedy to triumph. As this book was about to go to press, Jay O'Dell has now told his story of conversion in mind, body and spirit to thousands of youth and adults within the local community. He is a gifted teacher, preacher and expert in chemical addiction and the spiritual foundation which can lead an addicted individual to recovery from the same.

It is now a little over four years since James O'Dell jumped bail in Texas and was arrested in Mississippi at a motel off Interstate 10 in Bay St. Louis. In his possession were two pistols, heroin and he had warrants for his arrest from three counties in Texas. Since then James has become a daily inspiration to the jail staff and the inmate population who are blessed to sit under his teaching in the drug and alcohol treatment classes, which he provides to those suffering from chemical and cross addictions.

I was blessed to have met James within a few days of his arrest and get to know him while he was in the general population of the jail. Amazed at his knowledge of the depravity of the criminal mind and the story of his journey through every kind of rise and fall which a man could encounter in this life, I asked him to enroll in the first formal treatment course conducted at the jail in early 2019. To no one's surprise he was the valedictorian of his graduating class and has gone on to teach in the Chainbreakers drug and alcohol treatment program, while instructing in the Deliverance and Healing faith-based program also offered to inmates in the jail.

As you read James O'Dells story, do so by comparing his story with those who have now become the leading teachers in the field of treatment and recovery from addiction. His compelling writing style offers both hope for a better life in recovery, and a warning to those who have yet to yield to the demands which God's word levies upon every man and woman in their lifetime. Surrendering his life to the lordship of Jesus Christ has made all the difference in James Odell's life. He succinctly conveys the truth that a life wholly submitted to God, while loving one's neighbor as oneself, is the means through which true peace and joy can be found.

Come with me as we follow James Odell's story and meet a man who has learned what true freedom and peace is really about, and how to achieve both in your own life. As you read, see how James Odell's progression has followed a path similar to those of the giants in recovery, and how a knowledge of Bible teaching combined with the practical and spiritual tenets of the twelve-step program can transform your own life. I am honored to know James and see what God can do in a life fully ready to receive Him!

Dan Munger

# DEDICATION

To my mother, Emma Louise Bolton, and my father, James Earl Bolton. I want to thank you for doing the best you could on this side of Heaven to raise me to be an honest man—even though I got off track. I thank God you sent me to church when I was five years old. I know I will never see you again mom, on this side of Heaven. But, I know and believe we will meet again when I step from this life, through the doorway of death, to eternity, into all of God's glory. I love you mom. I will never forget your unconditional love. Thanks for being the best mom ever.

I would also like to dedicate this book to my three beautiful daughters. There hasn't been a day go by that I haven't thought about you in over two decades. I will always carry the memory of you with me in my heart. I hope one day to see you again. God bless you, and may the good Lord keep you safe until we meet again. You'll forever be in my heart.

# ACKNOWLEDGMENTS

When I was first asked to write this book. I never would have dreamed of what was about to occur for me when I committed to doing it. This book was written to shed light on God's goodness to the world, and demonstrate how he turned a sinner from the error of his ways. My purpose was to help people like me who once lived in utter hopelessness and despair without Jesus Christ as their Savior.

Like Elvis Presley said, "I did it my way." Sadly, my way never worked because the best I could do was give myself a life of mediocrity. My heart would never settle for second best because my God-given destiny is greatness. I thank God every day that He put it in my heart to live a life of abundance and store my treasure in Heaven. There is not a moment that goes by that I don't thank God for helping me to recognize I'm spiritually needy, and what I desire, above all things, is a relationship with him through Jesus Christ.

I could not have written this book without the help of Chaplains Dan and Joan Munger. I thank God for both of them every day. They are the kindest, sweetest souls on this side of Heaven. They are a prime example of to live is Christ and to die is gain. Thank you from the very bottom of my heart. I would also like to thank Brother Pat Burke. A couple of years ago, Brother Pat inspired me to be a testimonial speaker, and it was all to the glory of God. I thank God for that gift every day. I want to thank Sister Ann Burke for supporting her husband Pat Burke's prison ministry all these years.

I would also like to thank a very special friend of mine. Baby, you and I know who you are. Thank you for all of your help. I want to thank Jay and Rhonda Gamble. Through their perseverance in the last year, they have shown me that no matter what happens to you in life, if you're a child of God, it happens for you. Jay and Rhonda Gamble have taught me that at all costs, you must add value to the lives of those around you and do it to God's glory. Most importantly, Jay and Rhonda Gamble taught me that I must unconditionally trust the Lord with all my heart. They are a prime example of that in humanity. I believe and declare that God has turned Jay and Rhonda's tragedy into triumph, and all to his glory. I pray each day that the Lord will bless them beyond measure.

I want to thank Brother Tony. He is a genuine Christian with genuine Love for all of God's creation. Tony taught me that I shouldn't have to tell people that I'm a Christian, that they should know it by my love for them because God is Love and He is in me acting according to his will and good pleasure. Tony is a true friend beyond more than I could comprehend. A few years ago, Brother Tony taught me how to study the Bible intently. Coincidentally, it was of divine inspiration.

I want to thank the Hancock County Sheriff's Office for giving me the gift of true life. You have all been a shining example of compassion in my darkest hour. Thank you for treating me like a human being. You are all an inspiration to me. I want to thank everyone who treated me better than I ever could have dreamed. This includes C.I.D., Narcotics, Patrol, Records, and everyone else. God bless everyone who helped me along the way. Last but surely not least, my third wife Nicki, for thrusting me straight toward my God-given destiny. You had to make a lot of hard decisions to help me. Thank you from the depths of my soul. May you eternally rest in peace. I want to give a very special thanks to all the correctional staff at the Hancock County Jail. You are all my heroes.

# CONTENTS

# CHAPTER 1

## IN THE BEGINNING

I remember it like it was yesterday. I was five years old, lying on the floor next to my mother, asleep at approximately two o'clock in the morning. Suddenly, the living room door flew open. Then my father came bursting through the opening, home drunk again! Immediately, he began shouting obscenities at my poor mother, ranting and screaming! He stumbled around the room, glassy-eyed and incoherent. I was terrified because I didn't know what he might do. But my mother remained calm and sheltered me. She knew he would do us no harm. And surprisingly to me, he didn't even break a thing during his off-balance tirade. In fact, my mom knew my father would soon fall asleep and be snoring within five minutes. Fortunately, she was right. But unfortunately, this event was perfectly normal for my family.

I was going to leave this part of my life story out because I really respect my mother and father. But I needed to paint a crystal clear picture of what happened. Also, I need you to understand what it was that sent me down the path of destruction at such an early age. So please understand my mother and father were wonderful people. They were honest and hard-working people. But they were uneducated, and they lacked a lot of life skills. My mother was from California, and my father was from Ohio. My father couldn't read or write whatsoever. My parents had four children together, of which I was the oldest. And my mother had four children from another marriage. So my mother and father had eight children in all.

Growing up, my family was poor, and we lived on government-assisted living. When the food stamps ran out toward the end of every month, we would eat out of trash cans behind the local grocery stores. It was absolutely horrific. But I loved my parents beyond comprehension, and I swore as a young man I would never be poor when I was grown. Being poor, living in the ghetto, going to bed hungry a lot of nights, and having an abnormal home life profoundly impacted every aspect of my being. You know, as far back as I can remember, I never once felt loved, needed, or wanted.

## THE LACK OF THE LOVE OF MY FATHER

"The sins of the fathers fall on the sons."

My father only told me he loved me three times from age five until I was forty-one years old. Looking back now, I have learned that love is a person. And that person is the one and only true God of Abraham, Isaac, and Jacob. I know now that God's love is shown in action. The Apostle Paul described those actions in the Bible where he said, "Love is patient, love is kind, it does not envy, it does not boast, it is not rude, it is not self-seeking, it always trusts, hopes, endures, and preserves all things. Love never carries any record of wrongs, and love never fails" (1 Corinthian 13:4-8).

Love never fails because God is love, and God can't forget; it is impossible. In retrospect, I realize my parents loved me as best they could. In truth, I'm grateful to God for giving me the

14

parents he did. I wouldn't change that fact for any amount of money. So it was a constant struggle financially for my parents their entire lives.

As a child, I remember we moved a lot. We lived in motels on and off through the years and were unstable in many ways as a family. I often changed schools. Every time we would get comfortable, we'd move. Every time I would make friends, we were up and moving again. It was one struggle after another. I can only imagine how my parents felt. When I was six months old, my parents decided it would be best to leave Ohio and return to California, where my mother was from. But, as fate would have it, somehow, some way, they got lost because they couldn't read or write, so they couldn't read a map.

This was how my family wound up in the great state of Texas. I must tell you that the struggles of life are real. Once, we wound up broken down on the side of the road for two weeks. It was my mother, father, four older brothers and sisters and me. I can only imagine how hopeless my parents felt in that situation. But God's grace proved sufficient. A Christian couple who lived nearby stopped one day while my father was at work just to see if we were okay. Can you picture my mother and her five children, one of them who was six months old, sitting on the side of the interstate in the 100-degree heat? That had to have been a hopeless feeling. The couple decided to come back when my father was there. They fixed our car and got us a motel room for two weeks. That work of mercy provided just enough time for my dad to get his first paycheck, enabling him to begin supporting us again.

## THE STRUGGLE WITHIN

Both of my parents worked, but the problem was they worked for next to nothing because they were uneducated. They couldn't help it; they did their best with the life skills they had. Needless to say, the only normality in my family was the abnormality. That took its toll on me very early on in life. My father and I were close, but my father was also a man's man. My grandpa General Lee Bolton was also a man's man and a moonshiner born in 1919. My grandpa lived a rough life, and by the ripe old age of 12, he was running moonshine up and down the river bank of Northeastern Tennessee. My grandfather was a drinker, my great-grandfather was a drinker, and my father was a drinker. So what might you think I became? Ding, ding, ding, ding, you guessed right, and I became an alcoholic by the age of 20. Incredibly, I had been abusing alcohol since I was twelve years old. The first drink I ever took was behind a convenience store in Arlington, Texas. I remember it like it was yesterday. My father handed me a quart of beer, and I drank it. He drank his, handed me some gum, and said, "Stay away from your mother; she will kill me if she finds out I gave you alcohol."

I didn't know it then, but that event would turn out to be the catalyst that led me down the path of self-destruction. You see, my father was a hard drinker. In other words, he could drink one or one thousand beers, and he could also take it or leave it. As for me, I always, from the first day of my drinking, had a major problem with drinking to excess. So, as I walked back home with my father on the day I took my first drink, I distinctly remember wanting another one. It was as if my body was screaming, "Give me another drink." It's essential for you to understand something. There were three generations before me who were functioning alcoholics and hard drinkers. There were two who had died from the side effects of alcohol abuse on the human body. Further, I didn't know at the time, but when you abuse alcohol and drugs before eighteen, you are sixty-five percent more likely to use other drugs and become addicted. The first time I used illicit drugs, I was twelve years old. The first drug I ever used was cocaine. I liked the effects of cocaine, but I wanted the effects of alcohol more, and it was easier for me to get.

So, in retrospect, alcohol and cocaine were probably my gateway intoxicants to crime. The next thing you know, I'm carrying a pistol at twelve years old! I then met some older guys who started using me as a pawn in their auto theft ring. We would steal multiple cars a night, sometimes as many as six! Then, they would take the cars to local body shops, which were run by thieves. They often call them "chop shops" because they would exchange parts on cars there, change the vehicle identification number, and then file for lost titles. Then most of the time, these stolen vehicles were shipped to Mexico to be sold to the criminal underworld. During the day, we also burglarized houses. We stole anything of value that we could sell. I quit school within four months of being involved in this auto theft ring. And, within six months, all of us were busted! Some of us were tried as adults, and some as juveniles. In the end, it didn't matter, and the judge gave all of us time. All the adults went to prison. But, I was put on trial as a juvenile and found guilty of burglary and auto theft. I was sentenced to one year at Buckner's Baptist Boys Ranch in Burnett, Texas. That was in 1990, and all of this occurred within six months of my first drink of alcohol!

## AN OPPORTUNITY TO MEET MY MAKER

When I got to the boys' ranch, it was a very structured environment. There were about 20 children that were assigned to two adults. We called them house parents. Most of them were old retired couples. They were good people with a genuine love for us. I had some behavioral problems, but I did well in school. However, the sum of the things that had been going on in my life started to take a toll on my soul. I began developing a warped perception of life and how I viewed people, places, and things. And this skewed perception of life led me to have a profoundly negative impact on my thought processes and the way I made choices. The saving grace was that the boys' home made us go to church. I remember it was a Baptist church, which was good because my mother made me go to church when I was only five years old. It was Trinity Baptist Church in Arlington, Texas.

I liked going to church and it was good for me. One day I was sitting in the second pew of the church, and God spoke to me and said, "I want you to be a preacher." I didn't know it was the Holy Spirit speaking to me at the time. But a few days later, on August 17, 1991, at approximately nine o'clock in the morning, at Buckner's Baptist Boys Ranch, I bowed my head, recited the sinner's prayer, and converted to Christianity. The reason for my conversion was simple: I didn't want to burn in hell. I wanted blessings and prosperity, I wanted a mansion in the sky, and I wanted to walk on streets paved with gold so pure you could see through them. You get the point; I became a Christian for all the wrong reasons! Looking back now, what is amazing to me, is that while I called myself a Christian from the time I was twelve years old until I was forty-one, I faithfully served myself and the god of this world (Satan), all the while believing I was faithful to the Father, Son, and Holy Spirit. And, during that time, I never exhibited any Christ-like behavior, both of which tell me I did not come to a *"Godly sorrow which brings repentance that leads to salvation without regret" (2 Cor. 7:10).*

So my profession of faith had been a sham. I remember believing I was saved because I said the so-called sinners' prayer. I know now that isn't true. The power of self-deception wreaked havoc on my soul and opened doors that I wouldn't be able to close for the next twenty-nine years on my road of self-sufficiency. It was terrible; you can't imagine in your wildest dreams the depths to which my sin problem would take me. I mean, think about this, how could a young, innocent twelve-year-old boy become so terribly misled and misunderstood?

During my life from five to forty-one years old, I never once felt loved, needed, or wanted. That is a horrible thing for any child to have to go through. No one, especially a child, should ever feel like that! I felt left behind, isolated, alone, tormented, oppressed, and depressed. I didn't know what to do. I felt like I was broken on the inside. I felt like God was distant, that he had forgotten about me, and that I wasn't worthy of being loved. Sometimes I felt like I was the only person on the planet. I felt like I was all alone, and I was full of fear. Everything I did was motivated by fear. If God existed, and he was the God of all comfort, why on earth did I feel so uncomfortable, so afraid? How come every time someone tried to love me, I couldn't give or receive love? What had I done to deserve to feel as I did when I was twelve? Even at forty-one years old, I still felt like this. I also felt like a boy trapped inside a man's body. Trying to make it in a dog-eat-dog world!

## SEX, ALCOHOL, AND COCAINE

It was in 1992, at the ripe old age of fourteen, I left the boys' ranch and went home. Although I was only sentenced to one year, I decided to stay for two years. A couple of years later, my brother John asked me to come home. It was at the advice of my oldest brother John I decided to go back home against my better judgment. John, who himself had been released from prison a year earlier. He was also all too familiar with a troubled childhood. He also turned to drugs and a life of crime. But John quickly came to his senses and corrected his behavior. He was a very smart man for doing that. He was also the only constant positive impact at the time in my life. He did his best, but couldn't beat my genetics and epigenetics. I heard William Shakespeare say, "The sins of the fathers fall on the sons." My brother John was ten years older than me, and John was my favorite brother. He saw what I was going through. He also remembered exactly what he had gone through. Through his experience, strength and hope, John tried to stop me from going down the wrong path. But when I got back home from the boys' ranch, I went to live with my parents. Sadly, within a few months, I was completely out of control. I was drinking, doing cocaine, and had become sexually active.

Then when I was fourteen, John tried to swoop in and save me. My brother had a great job and a nice car and lived in a great neighborhood. He saw that I was failing living with my parents, so he took me to live with him. He could see that my situation at the time was a recipe for disaster. He knew the way I was headed would end in one of three ways: trouble with the law, killing someone, or being killed. John was the only one who could see I was out of control. The best way to describe what happened is that my normality was the epitome of absolute abnormality. I was completely and utterly dysfunctional. There was nothing normal about me! I had become the epitome of terrible cognitive behavior. Every thought, emotion, attitude, and action was a composite of bad choices. At that point, I was completely bankrupt as a human being and had nothing to give humanity.

# THE DAY I ALMOST LOST MY LIFE

So at fourteen years old my life became so bad that one of the local street gangs put a hit out on me. It was all over a girl I had dated for a short period. She started dating one of the gang's leaders when we broke up. Well, she and I had broken up on bad terms. So, she lied to the gang leader and said I had bragged that I was going to "Shoot him on sight." Further, she also failed to tell him I was just fourteen years old.

I was walking with a good friend named Jeff early one evening. Jeff and I had known each other since we were five years old. It was getting dark when a black Monte Carlo pulled up on us with three Latinos. I've got a .25 caliber semi-automatic nickel-plated pistol in my pocket, loaded, and got one in the chamber. They drove past us as we were walking the other way. I heard a car door slam shut. As I turned around to look back, I was shocked; there was a large caliber pistol in my face. The young man asked, "Who are you?" I told him. Then the weirdest thing happened, the Latino male holding the pistol in my face asked, "How old are you?" I quickly told him, "14." He scolded me and instructed me to stop making threats, but when I look back, I see he realized I was barely a teenager. What he didn't know was that my gun was not only cocked and loaded, and my finger was on the trigger during our conversation. I also had a very baggy pair of JNCO jeans on, and I could have shot him at any time. But thank God for his love, grace, and mercy. Also, I thank God for putting enough mercy and sense into that young man's heart that he didn't kill me. That gang was the most violent street gang in Arlington, Texas, at the time. Afterward, my good friend Jeff and I walked back to his grandma's house so I could change my shorts; only kidding!

The really sad part was that Jeff was much worse off than I was, family-wise. His mother had substance abuse problems. His parents divorced or split up when he was young. His father was nowhere to be found. Their house was in ruins. It was terribly sad looking back now. I now know Jeff and his sisters never had a chance to become anything but statistics. In her defense, Jeff's mother did everything she could to steer her children the right way. But, as fate would have it, Jeff and his two sisters all grew up addicted. Sadly, they all went to prison.

## SUZANNE

By this time in my life, I had already met and was sexually active with a young girl named Suzanne. Suzanne would later become the mother of my two oldest daughters. We were together from the ages of sixteen to twenty-one. The first night I slept with this fourteen-year-old girl, I was sixteen. She got pregnant shortly after that. A couple of months later, she had a miscarriage. We got together because Suzanne's mother, Denise, was trying to get into a relationship with my brother John, whom I lived with at the time. What a fiasco! It was a three-ringed circus. In no time, Suzanne and I had become dangerously co-dependent upon one another, if you can imagine that! In addition, our relationship became abusive, unhealthy, and altogether horrific. When it was bad, it was worse. When it was good, it was great. The reason things were becoming so toxic between us stemmed from the fact that I was losing the fight with alcohol. My drinking had become more frequent, my drinking sprees ran closer together, and I always drank to excess! Suzanne noticed this, and because of my drinking, we fought constantly. I mean, I know she loved me the best way she knew how. But, it is terrible to watch your loved one slipping away to self-medicating gone wrong, watching them live a life of selfishness and self-centeredness, and a life that was nothing more than a composite of bad choices. That had to have been horrible for her to endure.

So here I am playing house with this 14-year-old girl, under the supervision of my brother John and Suzanne's mother, Denise. Wow! That is as insane as it gets! It is just shocking to me that the adults around Suzanne and I utterly failed us from every angle, completely and absolutely! It wasn't long after this time that my brother John's relationship with Suzanne's mother, Denise, took a turn for the worst. In fact, their relationship was probably ten times worse than Suzanne's and mine. Suzanne's mother, Denise, was getting a divorce from Suzanne's stepdad. She used the unsubstantiated claim that she caught Suzanne's stepdad *in the act* with another man as her excuse to end the marriage. I think Denise used that allegation to justify the relationship she and John were in. Wow! I told you it was a three-ringed circus. Then on top of all of this, poor Suzanne, who never knew her real dad, is not only losing her stepdad, but I'm slowly drinking more and more, more often and more frequently. In other words, with all the abnormal things going on in my life, the way I coped was that I consumed a lot of alcohol and had a lot of sex. Neither one is appropriate or normal for a sixteen-year-old! I mean here I was, this sixfteen-year-old child, trying to find his way in life, having already become a statistic. I continued to spiral out of control, straight toward the gates of a self-induced torturous hell. I'm sure by now it must be pretty easy for you to see how the first sixteen years of my life made me a prime candidate to become a liar, cheat, thief, con, and master manipulator. Sadly, to sum it all up, I was the absolute epitome of selfishness and self-centeredness.

# CHAPTER 2

---◆◆◇◆◆---

# TOTAL DEMORALIZATION

I was spiraling out of control, but I was desperately trying to find my way in life. My relationship with Suzanne, the future mother of my two oldest daughters, was getting worse. But, I knew the Ten Commandments. I'm sure you've heard of at least a few of them, like, thou shall not lie, steal, kill, or commit adultery. But it's important for you to understand that God puts the Natural Law in our hearts. And the Natural Law, upon which the Ten Commandments are based, is defined as *"The light of understanding, put in the human heart by God, which tells us what we must do, and what we must avoid."* And that understanding, if we follow it, will lead us to mirror God's righteousness. Simple huh? As I said previously, at God's prompting, my mother made me go to church starting when I was five years old. This is kind of amazing, considering my mother and father only went to church two times in my entire life. But thanks be to God because He knew what he was doing. The good Lord was molding me for greatness.

You see, God knew what I didn't at the time, *"I was his workmanship, created in Christ Jesus to do good works, which he prepared for me to do in advance"* (Eph: 2:10). The one and only true God, who is the creator of the universe and is a sovereign Lord, in control of all things, at all times, in all of creation, had a plan! You see my friend, God knew my future was so bright that I probably should have been born wearing sunglasses. God knows the future that He predestined for you and I before we were formed in the womb. So there is no doubt looking back now, that God put the idea in my mother's heart to send me to church.

Years later, I now believe wholeheartedly that I would be dead had my mother not made that decision to arrange that I be confronted with the Gospel. At best, I would be spiritually dead because I wouldn't know Christ as my savior. Therefore, my life now would at best, be one of mediocrity. Mediocrity is settling for second best and why would anyone have a good life? When God wants you to have an abundant life, a life crowned with a sense of purpose, joy, peace, and contentment? The truth is God wants to bless you exceedingly, abundantly, above and beyond all you could ask, think, or imagine! Having learned what I know now and knowing what I didn't understand then, the simple fact is that God taught us through the ten commandments vertically how to have a relationship with him and horizontally how to have a relationship with other people. Further, if one were to draw those lines on paper, they would make a cross due to their mutual dependence. To learn how to truly have good relationships. We must have a relationship with God through Jesus Christ first. We must come to the Author of unconditional love, which is God. We must do this in order to truly understand how to love God, ourselves, and our fellowman. You can't love God and not love your fellow man, his creation. Listen to this very carefully. The Bible says, "Greater love hath no man than this, that a man lay down his life for his friends" (John 15:13). When Jesus Christ died on the cross, He set an example for us to live by. To put it another way, relationships make a person's life meaningful. Jesus died on the cross so that He could restore our broken relationship with God.

I believed in my former life that I didn't need relationships; I only needed money. Simply put, the ten commandments teach us how to have a relationship with God and each other.

## CAREER CHOICES

So now having reached the ripe old age of sixteen, I started working with my brothers in the roofing industry. We were tearing off roofs in the heat of summertime. I was getting paid twenty dollars a day! It was brutal working in the heat. When we weren't doing roofing jobs, we were doing remodeling jobs; it all paid the same for me. Then, by the time I was sixteen years old, I had dropped out of school finally and forever. I took a job with a nationally known grocery store and somewhat cleaned up my act on the drinking side. In other words, I went on a dry drunk and tried to fight addiction on sheer willpower. Unfortunately, one's willpower alone seldom works because my lack of willpower led me down the path of self-destruction in the first place. This particular period of sobriety lasted about four months, and then I reverted to my old behavior. My brother Brandon showed up at my job one day and said, "You're making four twenty-five an hour here; I've got you a new job making seven dollars an hour working with me. I'll be your supervisor."

I quit my job at the grocery store and went home. At this point in my life, I started learning about self-sufficiency and how a man makes his own way. My life would come to be all about me soon after learning this. I had been taught to lie, cheat, steal, and manipulate my surroundings to get what I wanted! Every day I woke up, I had two things on my mind, to get this and to get that. I never gave anything to anyone without the intent of getting something back. I knew the world met nobody halfway; if you wanted something, you took it. That is exactly what I set out to do! I used and abused the people in my life to get what I wanted. Suzanne, the mother of my two oldest daughters, had become a doormat to me. I walked all over her and to make matters even worse, Suzanne got pregnant again. I kept drinking, and I kept using people to get things. Then, by the time I was seventeen, I had become a father. Sadly, I still had no parenting skills, and consequently, I missed out on a host of blessings because I wasn't willing to be the type of father to even get on the floor and play with my kids. Sadly, I treated my kids exactly like I was treated by my father.

Once again, I want to emphasize something. Throughout my youth, I never felt loved, needed, or wanted. Having never received love from my earthly father, I was unable to give love to others. The truth was, love was something that I knew very little about. It was terrible and I was emotionally detached from life itself because of this factor. I only cared about myself and what I wanted. Looking back now, it is kind of sad! I had no moral compass or any boundaries for my behavior at that point in my life. At the same time, I was definitely exhibiting all the earmarks of an addict, which were leading me to live a double life, one of a pathological liar and a master manipulator. But to complicate matters further, my brother's boss asked me one day, "If I thought I could sell remodeling jobs." He said, "I believe you could make a lot of money in remodeling." So that sounded great! I was eighteen years old and going nowhere fast, so I agreed to sell jobs for him.

# Robert

"A fool and his money soon part."


So my new boss, Robert, was the owner of a business that had been around since 1964. He was a very smart man. He liked to focus on only doing remodeling jobs. My new boss preferred remodeling jobs over roofing because remodeling also kept him busy in the winter time. It is a seasonal job in North Texas to work in the roofing business. Robert had me mainly focus on selling custom decks, cedar patio covers, and room additions. The good thing was that I had done the labor end of these trades for a couple of years. This factor made it very easy for me to sell the jobs and become a skilled estimator. My new boss had made millions of dollars remodeling apartments in the 1980s. He had two six-car garages full of custom corvettes; all show cars. These cars had 5-point S.I. certified diamonds in the shifters. They also had 24-karat gold engines in them. My new boss lived in a $500,000 house in Pantego, TX. He wore diamond rings on every finger and he carried around anywhere from fifty to one hundred thousand in cash all the time.

One day Robert looked at me and asked, "Where do you want to be in ten years?" I simply replied, "I want to be a millionaire." Robert said, "Son, with your talent and your looks, you will probably make more money than I have ever made." I was shocked! But he was dead serious and Robert never batted an eye. It was right there, at that moment, that something happened to me on the inside. That was the game-changer for my whole life. When he told me that, it was as if something deep down inside of me said, "You can be the best at what you do." Then out of nowhere, in the next six months, I went from making twenty dollars a day to making ten thousand dollars a month.

To his surprise, Robert couldn't believe I was selling so many jobs. Oh yeah, did I forget to mention? I only got paid if I sold the job. In other words, I got paid by commission only. I started making a good amount of money and to reward myself. I went out and bought eight diamond rings, one to put on every finger. Then I went right back to working fourteen to sixteen hours a day. Wow, let me tell you something, I was making money hand over fist. It was like I was born to be a salesman.

It was crazy; It seemed like every job I estimated I sold. Actually, it was eight out of ten of them, which was unheard of for a kid of my age and lack of experience! It was like payday every day because whenever I brought Robert a check, he paid me in cash on the spot. There was no question in my mind or anyone elses mind that the poor boy from Arlington, Texas, had arrived. It was about this time that I bought a brand new truck, had diamond rings on every finger, opened two bank accounts, and was walking around carrying at least $5,000-$10,000 cash on me at all times. I often hid this money from my wife Suzanne at the time. I wasn't having financial problems anymore. But, at the same time, it was never enough! There was always something deep down inside that said, "There has to be more to life than just fine cars, fine women, and fine dining."

Although I was doing magnificently in my business life, I was never at home; I was not tending to my wife and daughter. At this point, I was a slave to sin and to my job. More importantly, the new "god" I served was the god of money and this world, Satan. But, at the time, I was quite alright with that. If only I had known then, what I know now. These two gods require everything of you, including your soul.

# THE CURSE OF THE GOD OF MAMMON

"The worst thing that ever happened to me"

One day Robert called me and told me to come over to the office. When I got there, Robert said, "I would like to introduce to you an old friend of mine." His name was Tom, and Robert introduced him as "The best contractor in the entire roofing industry." He told me that Tom chased hail storms and hurricanes all over the Midwest and Florida. In fact, Robert told me, "Tom has come here to make you an offer that you can't refuse, son." That's when Tom explained to me that he had heard a lot of good things about me. He told me that he was the general manager for a company out of Greenwood, Indiana. He then explained that he had come all the way from Wisconsin to make me the deal of a lifetime! It all sounded great, but I was a little hesitant.

Tom proceeded to put me on the phone with the owner of the company up in Indiana at the time. John quickly assured me that my wife, child, and I would never want for anything if I came to work for him in the Midwest. My home base would be Minneapolis, Minnesota. Why would I not take the offer? I agreed! It wasn't long after that the company gave me a brand new truck, cell phone, an apartment style condominium, and a good sum of cash as a sign-on bonus. Tom explained that selling roofing was ten times easier than selling remodeling, and I would make way over six figures, working six months a year. So I did what any smart kid would do and I stress the kid part. I loaded up my wife and daughter, with Tom and his wife Donna, we all then started driving up interstate 35w north towards Minnesota from my residence at the time in Arlington, Texas.

Approximately one thousand miles later, we arrived at our destination. It was March 21, 1998, and Bill Clinton was the president of the United States, and here I was, nineteen years old. I knew nothing about life, had no boundaries or life skills, and Satan was slaughtering me from every angle. A fool and his money will soon part.

The world was mine. When we got to Minnesota, I looked around and said, "Tom, what the heck man, we're in the middle of a blizzard!" He quickly shot back and said, "Don't worry kid, we will be ok in a few days." Sure enough, the twenty-one inches of snow that fell melted over the next few days, and that first week, we were climbing roofs. Needless to say, we were passionate about what we did. But who wouldn't be? The roofs and the people's insurance money were all that mattered. We weren't really concerned about helping people. We were there for the big money! And it was the kind of money we were making that most people can only dream about. The money we were making was money my mother, father, brothers, and sisters had never thought possible when we were eating out of trash cans and watching people get murdered in the slums where I grew up.

## TOM

Life is a struggle! But you struggle a lot less with money, right? Wrong! Tom and I started making $25,000 a month right from the start. A modern-day equivalent to that income would be $63,000.00 per month. That is the God's honest truth. Honestly, it was crazy. You can only imagine. During these storms, Tom and I became good friends. We worked hard, and we played even harder. I started wearing designer clothing. A twenty-dollar bill was considered spare change in my world. I was making a lot of money fast, but the only problem was that I was walking around with two major addictions, I was an alcoholic and a sex addict.

I then decided to complicate my life even further by feeding both my addictions. I became addicted to strip clubs! You see, the thing was, I was leading a double life. My business life was immaculate, but inside, I was as dead as a man in the grave. I was lost, stubborn, rebellious, vain, and outright conceited. On the inside, I felt so dirty and nasty that I had to put on this façade on the outside as a defense mechanism so nobody would be able to know my deepest darkest secrets. That is why I wore designer clothing, I had to drive a new truck, and why I had to wear diamond rings. That way, I could be distracted by external things, so I didn't have to deal with the pain in my heart. Just maybe, if I looked good enough on the outside, you might surmise I was the same on the inside. In the end, I realized I had no integrity, which was a terrible place to be in life. I had built walls so high around my heart that you couldn't get a helicopter to fly high enough to get inside of the walls around my heart. I was terribly broken and deceived. There was no way I was going to be hurt again! My mind had literally become the scariest neighborhood I had ever been in.

## SEXUAL ADDICTION AT ITS WORST

During that time, the town of Minneapolis, Minnesota, had the third-best strip club in the country. It was located in downtown Minneapolis. The women that worked there were top-of-the-line. Shortly after, a couple of times where I spent about $2,500 in one night, the strip club started compelling me to use a Limo or a Rolls Royce to get there, free of charge. I mean, this was an every night affair. It was insane. There were all white-collar businessmen there. Anywhere from accountants to stock brokers, real estate investors, the whole nine yards. Man, I spent so much money that people would ask me where I worked. I would tell them what I did, and they would shake their head in total disbelief and say, "I guess I'm in the wrong business." Tom and I would party until two in the morning on most nights. We would down our last drink in the parking lot of our condo, and I would have snorted my last line of cocaine off of a stripper's backside to be polite or from some other part of her body, but by about two o' clock in the morning we would usually head home. I was very sick at that point in my life. We were having sex with strippers in V.I.P. rooms at the club, their houses, and hosting parties that cost us a fortune everyweekend. It was craaaaaaaaaaaaaaaaaazy! It was also sad because our wives were being dehumanized, demeaned, and cheated on. They had done nothing wrong but try to love us.

So here I am, a nineteen-year-old kid from Arlington, Texas. I'm doing pretty well for myself. But, one of my major problems was that I was very selfish and morally and emotionally bankrupt. I knew right from wrong. I also knew I shouldn't have treated my wife that way. But nobody was going to tell me what to do. My wife was married to me, and I was married to everyone and everything but her. I was considered an Independent Contractor with the company I was working for. In other words, I got a W-9 form from the Internal Revenue Service, not a W-2 from the company. I paid my own taxes, and I was my own boss. I made my own schedule, I answered to the owner of the company, and that was when I wanted to. If I didn't like what he wanted me to do, I didn't do it. The reason being is that the company owed Tom and me a lot of money, and they would have to pay us if they fired us. So the sheer logistics of how we got paid was off of the profit margin, making it very complicated to fire Tom and me. The reason why was that it is nearly impossible to predict a job cost before it is completed.

It was by this time Tom and I were at the point in our careers where the company always owed us a lot of money. Additionally, we were their best sales representatives. In fact, we were so good that Tom and I, and eight other sales representatives, outsold fifty other sales representatives at a competing company. Upon hearing about us, the owner of that particular company and his sales representatives came over to meet with us to try to recruit us. Truth be told, we didn't have any interest in it. Our primary reason for staying where we were was that the company was known for "ripping off" its sales team. Further, we had a great thing going where we were. But we entertained their offer at the strip club, used them, got a free party for eight hours, and then told them no thanks three days later. We also realized the employees from the other company were bigger crooks than us. Therefore, Tom and I decided that if anyone was going to get scammed, it would not be us. But there was one thing for certain! Nobody was going to scam the scammers. I want you to understand something. Tom and I never tried to scam a homeowner. We were dishonest with insurance companies for homeowners by paying their deductibles and billing the insurance companies in full. We just got into many bad situations with the companies we worked for because we were told to do that. We also had a problem with idolizing money and had serious addictions and compulsions. Therefore we wound up making a lot of bad decisions regarding funds.

# MORALLY BANKRUPT

It was about this time that the storm was closed out. Tom and I ended up making about $220,000 a piece from the storm that blew through the Great Lakes, in about six months. Further, our hard work made John, the owner of that company, a multimillionaire that year, all from that hail storm. It's funny how life works out. Two years earlier, John, the owner of the company, was making $35,000 annually as a health teacher in Indiana. John took a chance with his life savings on two guys from Texas and won the roofing lottery. I'm laughing, but it is true. It still amazes me how my lifestyle during that run didn't affect my work ethic. But the really crazy part of all this was that people loved us, because we did exactly what we told the customers we would do. It was inarguable that the roofs we installed were the best in the business. The houses we re-roofed looked better than all the other houses in the neighborhood. We were master roofers; not only could we sell the jobs, but we could also do the jobs. And we did all our jobs according to the manufacturer's specifications. We were top-notch professionals. We were great at what we did, and we were the best residential roofing sales representatives in the country. There is truly no doubt about that fact. No one in the residential roofing sales industry made as much money as Tom and I at that time. That was a fact proven time and time again. We had also become one of the best-known and most respected companies in the business and sales team.

As I think back now if I had lived a better personal life and possessed more self-restraint, one of two things would have happened. I would have been a millionaire at least ten times over, or I probably would not know Jesus Christ as my savior today. As the millionaire, more than likely, I would have gone on to the bitter end using people to get things and die in my SIN PROBLEM! But as the transformed sinner now, I have come to believe the good Lord was protecting me somehow all along the immoral path I was following. At the time, with all the distractions, I couldn't see God's hand in my life. But there's no doubt in my mind, looking back now, that he was protecting me and guiding me as much as He could. The problem was my God-given free will had driven me to the brink of insanity and a self-induced torturous hell. This was mainly because of my addictions and compulsions.

I went back to my condo one day in 1998, and my wife Suzanne had left with our daughter. She was tired of my cheating, drinking, staying out all night, and besides that, I was a ghost husband. In other words, I paid the bills and had sex with her; other than that, I was a slave to my job, and my true marriage was to money, alcohol, and women. Suddenly as I looked up at the television set with tears in my eyes and took a real good look at the screen, I could see the impeachment trial of President Bill Clinton going on. I thought to myself, what in the world is wrong with my life? All the obvious problems were there, like cheating, drinking too much, not budgeting my money, and basically being irresponsible. But the real truth was that I was an addict. I had placed myself beyond the point of human aid. In other words, selfishness and self-centeredness were the roots of all my troubles. I had a sin problem, and as the scriptures say, "The wages of sin is death, but the free gift of God is eternal life in Christ Jesus our Lord" (Romans 6:23 ERV).

# TAKING STOCK OF MY LIFE

In retrospect, you could say I was at the stopping point or the last stop on the train. At that point, I could have found help and prevented further damage in my life. But, as fate would have it, the phone rang the next morning, and It was John, the owner of the company. My head hurt, and I was hungover. I looked over at a girl in my bed, half-naked. I didn't even know her name. Pitiful, how sad! John quickly said, "I flew in last night on my private plane." I said, "Private plane?" He said, "Yeah, I purchased it a month ago." John said, "You and Tom meet me at the airport; we're flying to Ohio a half of a billion-dollar hail storm just hit there." So just like that, Tom and I flew to Columbus, Ohio.

We flew to Columbus, Ohio, and landed. The weather during the flight wasn't good, it was a small plane, and we took a beating during the flight. I hated flying but didn't have a choice. But immediately, we went straight to the oldest roofing company in Columbus. In no time, we struck up a deal with them. It was the sort of deal that was done all the time in the roofing industry. We sheltered our company name, under the local company's name and became a division of their company, so if the customer didn't ask, we looked local. If they did ask, we were a large, nationally known roofing company opening offices in new markets around the country. We always made it look like we were a division of the local company. We would pay the local company anywhere from $300-$1,000 a job. That meant every job. Interestingly enough, we had all become unethical crooks. But, recalling that storm and others, the one thing we consistently did right was we did a great job every time—not good, great!

By this time, I was missing my wife Suzanne, and my daughter Alice. I was really tired. But, It was too early in my career to be tired. I needed a break for a moment. I then decided to drive to Oklahoma, where Suzanne was from. But when I got there, she quickly told me where I could go, and it wasn't to Heaven. But I begged and pleaded with her to go back to chasing hailstorms with me. She loved me, so she finally agreed and returned with me to living a storm chaser's lifestyle. Sadly, the love she had shown me over and over wasn't enough to get me to change my life. Suzanne had given me countless opportunities to become the sort of husband she wanted, and I knew I should be. I simply was still totally self-absorbed and *failed again to "Turn my will and my life over to the care of God as I understood Him" (World Services).* To top that off! She dropped a bombshell on me. She was pregnant again with our second child.

It wasn't long after a little more than a year in Ohio, and on the eve of my daughter's Brenda's birth, I left Columbus and told John that I was cashing out all my jobs. I settled for seventy cents on the dollar and went home. Looking back now, it was sad. I never did anything good with the money I earned during those years. *It was all cursed!* All the odds were against me: How I was raised, my genetics (generations before me were alcoholics and outlaws), I was suffering from a broken heart, and it was because my father never told me he loved me. That was one of the worst things that could have happened to me. That was the catalyst that set everything in motion. I really needed his validation. Even worse, I had never given my parents even a dime of the hundreds of thousands of dollars I wasted on chemicals and carnal pleasures. *I was a failure as a man, a husband, and a deplorable son. "Oh, what a wretched man that*

*I am, who can deliver me from this body of death?" (Romans 7:24).*

## TEXAS REVISITED, SEARCHING FOR ANSWERS

Our second daughter was born almost immediately after Suzanne and I returned to Texas. And you wouldn't believe it. A billion-dollar hail storm breaks out in the spring of the year 2000. It was kind of crazy because everyone a couple of months earlier was concerned with the computer glitch of 2000. Nevertheless, here I am, broken-hearted, living in the past, you know, "If only syndrome." *"If only I had done this or that."* And the converse, *"If only I hadn't done this or that."* All the while, I was drowning in a sea of money and alcohol-searching for something, but at the time, I wasn't quite sure what it was!

I remember telling my business partner one day that I felt like I was chasing a ghost. I didn't realize it at the time. But it was the Holy Ghost. I was making a fortune for a guy like me. I had a beautiful wife of which I had been with for six years, and I had two beautiful children. Last but not least, I had my piece of the American dream. But, the only problem was on the inside, I was as dead as a man in the grave. I had a rebellious spirit. I was destroyed in my heart from harboring unforgiveness, mainly toward my father for not validating that he loved me. I didn't know it at the time. But, if you don't forgive your neighbor for his trespasses, God will not forgive you. Unforgiveness is a sin unto death. The reason why is that you reap what you sow in this lifetime and the next. Then once you violate the word of God in that manner, you open the doorway of your soul to not only the spirit of unforgiveness, but to bitterness, anger, hatred, retaliation, violence, and murder—

40

whether it is in your heart or physically. God weighs the motives of a man's heart. These are just a few of the things that my heart was full of back then.

I also had another major problem back then. The first and foremost was a love problem. I hadn't been taught how to give and receive love appropriately by my family. In other words, in the manner that God loves you and I. Unconditionally! I also didn't know that God loves us for who we are and where we're at, not by what we do. You see, Jesus Christ came and died for us while we were still sinners, and it is by this, my good friend, that "God showed how much he loves us" (Romans 6:8). You see, my main problem (the love problem) only God could fix. My whole life, I tried to earn my father's affection; if only I could make good grades and be good enough, then maybe he would love me. A conditional human watered-down, distorted version of what love is supposed to be like, the love that the god of this world sells people, a conditional love. That always leaves them high and dry, sells them short in life, and that love is a complete and absolute distortion of the truth. The truth is that God loves us unconditionally. My father, not validating he loved me, had caused me to harbor unforgiveness in my heart. I did this all out of ignorance of the word of God. The lack of the truth of God's word almost killed me.

I wish I had known then what I know about the Bible now. I wish I had known that God understands our brokenness as no one else can, and He has already made provision to heal our sin problem through the one and only Lord of Lords and King of Kings. That would be through his son Jesus Christ. It is through the sacrificial death, burial, resurrection, and ascension of Jesus to the right hand of the Father, that blessed, saved, sanctified, redeemed, justified, and delivered us into God's glory! But, at the time, I didn't understand that.

# THE WORST MISTAKE I EVER MADE

Then to complicate my life even more. I went to the store one morning to buy a pack of cigarettes. I walked past the beer cooler and couldn't resist. I proceeded to drink about a six-pack of beer. However, I knew Suzanne would be very angry if I smelled like alcohol when I got back home. I then decided I was tired of fighting with her about my drinking. I went back home and got dressed and when I went to walk out the door, I paused for a brief second and looked at Suzanne and my kids lying there sound asleep like angels; I began to cry. Then I just walked away at 21 years old, and it was over. I left because I needed another drink.

I tried to get back together with her a few months later. But it was too late! She politely told me where to go. Today, I say good for her, realizing I deserve all the suffering I have experienced because of all the suffering I caused Suzanne. She didn't deserve anything she got from me. The harvest she reaped from all those years she spent with me was one of pain, and it was all my fault. I have only spoken with her a handful of times in the last twenty years. Maybe just maybe, one day, the good Lord will allow us to cross paths and somehow, some way, I will be able to make amends to her. But until then, I will be making amends to everyone else I ever had a negative effect on by glorifying God with my life. One thing I am sure about though, is that Suzanne and my daughters will stay on the top of that list until I can ask her to forgive me for the damage I caused her and our children!

# 21 YEARS OLD, ON THE ROAD TO NOWHERE

So after Suzanne told me where to go, I went crazy! I had more money than I knew what to do with. The hail storms kept coming every spring like clockwork, and so did the stacks of one-hundred-dollar bills. I started making an average of about $225,000 a year. By that time, I also had a whole baseball team full of women. So here I am, twenty-one years old, pushing twenty-two years old and making the kind of money most people never even dream of. At that time, I was sleeping with a different woman every night. One time I was held up in a high-end hotel, more like a resort, and I slept with three women in one day. It was terrible, but hey, at least I knew their names. That sounds funny, but the sad, disgusting truth is that I was famous for not knowing a woman's name.

One night I pulled into a strip club in Arlington, Texas. I was in a Hummer Stretch Limo, and it seated sixteen people. You can almost stand up in a Hummer. I rented all my limos out of Dallas, Texas. I had a driver from Italy named Giovanni. They would cost me $2,400 a night. I would only take them if I were alone. They would make a very bold statement when I drove up. I would always have a one hundred dollar bill folded perfectly in my hand, so when I shook the manager's hand, I would hand it off. Most of them knew me as Jay. I would immediately tell the manager, "I want this girl, that girl, oh and this one too. I want them back here in the V.I.P. room with me." I would specifically instruct him to have one bouncer outside the V.I.P. room. I would pay him $50.00 an hour. Iwould also instruct my driver Giovanni to be the second bouncer, andask him to let all the women know this was a party by invitation only. I would pull out a bag of cocaine, chop up four lines, and blow the first one; I would pass the tray, and if any of the girls didn't snort cocaine, I would throw them out of the party. It was crazy! It got so bad at one point that I had nine girls who were sitting there with me. I was throwing money around like I was a billionaire. You have to understand something; these girls treated me just like I treated my customers, like a dollar sign. I provided great service, and I got paid very well. Likewise, they also provided service and got paid a fortune! That particular night I spent at least $3,600. I was addicted to the lifestyle. But, the real allure for me was, in a strip club, there were no clocks, a lot of alcohol, it was dark, there was music, and last but surely not least, many naked women. I needed to escape from the truth, and the truth was that I was sick and self-destructive.

You see, that was my escape from reality. The crazy thing was that with the money I was making, I could have slept with any girl I wanted, but dealing with stress through carnal distractions was very sick and self-destructive, and that was the only way I knew how to cope with what I had become. The book of life is brief, once the final page is read, all but love is dead, and this is my belief. I was searching to be loved in all the wrong places! The saddest thing is that as I look back now. There I was in the biggest limo I could find at the time, with five bank accounts, anywhere from $15,000-$25,000 cash on me at all times, diamond rings on each hand, major credit cards, a career—not a job—new trucks, new Cadillacs, fine women, and fine dining. But I was the loneliest man on the planet.

## A NEW WIFE, BUT NOT A NEW LIFE

There was something elusive that I desperately needed, but I couldn't find it, and I couldn't buy it either. If I could have bought it, I would have had it instantly. It was like I was always wanting and wanting more. I was the epitome of selfishness, self-centeredness, greed, materialism, and a glutton. You have to understand that is exactly what having a sin problem does to you. It takes you further than you ever intended to go, makes you stay longer than you ever intended, and ultimately makes you pay more than you ever intended. In the end, our sin problem kills us, and God makes that possible through the gift of free will. God doesn't punish us. We do that to ourselves. The Bible says, "The wages of sin is death, but the free gift of God is eternal life in Christ Jesus our Lord" (Romans 6:23, ESV). I didn't know this at the time because I was on the road of self-sufficiency and self-destruction.

But that was my main problem, *self!* Selfishness and self-centeredness were, in fact, the root of all my troubles. In retrospect, my problems were all of my own makings. But I couldn't see that at the time. Remember when I told you I stepped over my two daughters, looked at my wife Suzanne, and began to cry? Well, it turns out that mortally wounded me. It got so bad between the women in my life and self-medicating gone wrong (alcohol and drugs) that life became one big sea of delusion. It was sad and there I was God's creation, but I was idolizing women, money, and on top of all that. I was drinking myself to death. Most of these things occurred because I couldn't live with myself for walking out on my two oldest daughters. All women at that point in my life were pawns to be used by me. So, what did I do? Another hail storm hit the

Dallas/Ft. Worth metroplex, and yet again, I dove headfirst into a sea of money.

But after I worked hard to earn as much money as possible, there would always come the alcohol and women. I have to tell you that I lived a great life! But, when it was bad, it was worse. When it was good, it was great! The reality was the money was always great. But I mismanaged every penny of it. Money, money, money. That was what my life was all about. That was the solution to all my problems, right? No, it wasn't in the very least bit. The money was cursed because I idolized it. Money was my false sense of security. But a fool and his money are soon parted. So, this is how it always went. I made a little less than $225,000 a year, but I lived like a millionaire while I was making other people literal millionaires in the roofing industry. To be sure, people in the roofing industry used me as much as I used them. I had a reputation for being a cash cow, a real go-getter, and a great earner. When a big storm hit, I would eat, sleep, and breathe roofing day and night! It was one of the best of my time. I could be ready to go with a team of sales representatives, trucks, trailers, and a rolling office, in a couple of hours. I could look at the direction the hail storm came in, the velocity of the storm, the path of the storm, how big the storm was, the population of the area affected, the average household median income of the people affected, and within 8 hours of scouting that storm, I would dissect it, and tell the owner of the company the best approach to get rich quick. I was like a general dissecting enemy territory so he could prepare troops for battle. The deep pockets in the roofing business paid me to protect their investment, and it all began and ended with me.

The roofing industry is a cut-throat business! Sometimes we would send spies from our company to other companies that we were in a bidding war with on a big commercial job. The sales representative would be working for us, but acting as if he worked for the other company. We'd steal their price list, see what their approach was to selling jobs, and where they were working at. Then the undercover rep would bring back that information to me, and I would give a counter-offer to the client, giving them more stuff for free, a better roof, or all the above. It was wild, and it was dirty too! Make no mistake, roofing is an unethical business that breeds unethical people. The saying was, "If all else fails, become a roofing contractor and get rich." Roofing was a tough business where only the strong survive. Sometimes, we would have two or three different company names, and we would send a number of different salesmen under different company names to give the client two or three different bids, each of those estimates being in the ballpark of the other. So, in the end, high or low, one of our estimates would get the job. The almighty dollar was the god we served! It was horrible and it was very unethical. But, it's a tough business, and one of the main problems was that hail storms could happen anywhere, and every storm chaser in the roofing industry is a player, if the storm is big enough. If not, we'd just call it a "local yokel" storm and wait for the next really big one!

## STAYING LOCAL

It was around 2002, and I was twenty-four years old. I realized Suzanne, the mother of my two daughters isn't ever coming back. So I decided to take it easy for a while. I stayed home locally and took a job as the General manager for a big construction company. They paid me a salary, a commission on my sales, and a 5% override on every job sold in the company. I controlled my drinking in a sense, but if you have to control something like drugs and alcohol. It is probably safe to say it is already out of control. Not surprisingly, the company I was the general manager for was a roofing and remodeling company. On a particular contract, I sold a room addition for them with a 40% profit. But, a few weeks later, my employer backed out of the contract. This was both unethical and illegal. The customer was livid and ended up suing me, the company, and the owner of that company. They sued us for everything but slipping on a banana peel. Six months later, after filing a written answer for the lawsuit through my attorney, the judge threw my part of the case out. It wasn't until my part of the lawsuit got dropped that I realized I got sued for nothing. I barely survived the suit and didn't make a penny in the process. That's construction for you!

Now it's the spring of 2003, and George W. Bush was the president of the United States. Our country was at war in Afghanistan and Iraq. The war on terrorism began right after September 11, 2001. I can still remember country superstars singing songs about 9/11. But as fate would have it a hail storm went right through my hometown. And It was huge! This thing was twenty-five miles wide, sixty miles long, from Weatherford to Rockwall, Texas. It was a billion-dollar hail storm! At the time in Texas, there had only been one bigger hail storm on record; on May 5th, 1995.

This is important because I'm about to complicate my life further and marry again, this time to a nurse I had met. Her uncle owned a roofing company, probably the largest independently owned roofing company in America! He got his big payday off the aforementioned 1995 hail storm. That storm would later propel him to recover from a life plagued with bad decisions to a $50,000,000 a year business with at least a thirty percent profit margin. So, I met his niece Lynn by chance and married her in 2003. As it turns out, Lynn's uncle died of lung cancer that year. But, he left Lynn and her son well over half of a million-dollar trust.

Lynn was a nice girl. And she was a career nurse by profession. She was not close to the uncle's part of the family. But her uncle blessed Lynn and her son regardless. That was good for her. I didn't need her money, so I started my own roofing company.

So now I have remarried and started my own business. All this occurred over one year. I knew Lynn for a mere 30 days when we got married. WOW! I went back to making money hand over fist because that had become second nature. By this time, I really couldn't understand how people could be poor. Money was so easy for me to make back then. The only problem I had with money was that I never saved a dime! I had money, nice things, and enjoyed the finer things in life at considerable expense. And while I presented myself to the world as an up-and-coming young businessman, inside, I was bankrupt as could be imagined; mentally, physically, emotionally, and spiritually. I could point to nothing which made my life seem worthwhile. Sadly, my life was devoid of any healthy and meaningful relationships. I lived for two reasons only. The first was to make an extraordinary amount of money. The second was to party. That was the vicious cycle I kept going through. The god of money was to whom I bowed, and it was pitiful. I amassed a small fortune with my own company. But, not content with the status quo, Lynn and I moved to the West Side of Ft. Worth, buying a 3,000-square-foot condo where you could step out the front door and play golf. The sad part about all this was that my life had devolved into living at a strip club seven nights a week, working seven days a week, and never being home.

Not surprisingly, Lynn filed for divorce nine months after we were married. Unbelievable, you say? Well, what should I have expected? I married this girl and hadn't even known her for more than thirty days! To top it all off, we both shared in that bad decision. I mean, why would anyone get married thirty days into a relationship? Insanity, my friend, absolute insanity! So, Lynn and I went to divorce court and were going to split everything down the middle. But Lynn and I decided she would get everything except the roofing business. It was over, and as I walked out of her attorney's office one day, I stopped, looked back, and said to her, "Don't worry, honey, someone still loves you, but I don't." I never saw or talked to her again. At the time she had been married and divorced five times.

I then proceeded to go back to making money hand over fist again. The only problem was that my drinking sprees had escalated to binge drinking. I used cocaine so I could stay up longer and drink more. I started blacking out, and I couldn't remember the next day what I had done the night before. I would do stuff people would tell me about when I was sober, which was very embarrassing. I started using the women I was with to nurse me after drinking sprees. Looking back, I needed help desperately. But the only problem was I bathed in the river of denial every day. I could always rationalize and justify my actions no matter what happened. The power of self-deception is not a good thing in the least bit. I was greatly deceived. People were concerned. My drinking and stinking thinking were affecting every area of my life. I was lost; I couldn't find my way in life. It didn't matter what I chose to do. My whole world was caving in on me. Here it was years later. I had been through one divorce, and I still wasn't over my first wife, who technically wasn't my wife at all. We were never married. But Suzanne and I had two daughters, and we'd been in a relationship for seven years. So, I feel like I would disrespect her by not calling her my wife. I was at the point where I would either wave the white flag and get into recovery or die the last man standing. I chose the latter.

## THE INEVITABLE COLLAPSE

I finally started getting in trouble with the law. I got my first D.U.I. At first, it was a slap on the wrist. Then, I got in a few bar fights and caught some assault charges. But I would always be able to buy my way out of trouble, and it was minor stuff anyway. Then, about the same time, I met a girl named Melanie. She was a contractor in the roofing industry herself. But Melanie was also a catastrophe adjuster. Melanie and I met one day through my ex-business partner Tom. Well, Melanie and I hit it off really well. The only problem was we were drinking and partying all night long. We had a lot of fun, but it turns out she was three months pregnant with another man's baby when we met.

But I loved Melanie so much (*being a bit sarcastic*). And the truth was, *I wasn't capable of loving myself because I didn't know how. So how in the world could I love anyone else?* We did well for a while. But I was not willing to be tied down by one girl. I went straight back to living in the strip clubs five nights a week and working seven days a week. I helped Melanie sell jobs because she was pregnant and my girlfriend. I've got to tell you. I was as fond of Melanie as you can get without loving somebody!

Melanie was an adjuster for a nationally known insurance company also. In 2005, a couple of years after I met Melanie, we were still together, and she got the call to be in Atlanta, Georgia, so when Hurricane Ivan blew in and hit the gulf coast, she could respond and adjust claims on the damaged property. Then here I am, I was living on the road off and on, and Melanie wanted me to go with her to help her adjust her claims. I reluctantly agreed because I needed some time off to pull myself together. I got my ex-business partner Tom to do all my jobs, and Melanie and I made our way to Atlanta, Georgia. Melanie was a catastrophe adjuster for Allstate Insurance company through an independent adjusting firm named Pilot Catastrophe Services. We waited three days, and Hurricane Ivan hit Pensacola, Florida, as a category three hurricane and destroyed it. We were on the ground on the fourth day in Pensacola. I had never worked in a hurricane. I quickly devised a get-rich-quick scheme, and I stress the scheme partly because I'm not at liberty to speak about it. Be that as it may, I called Tom and said, "Get down here. This is a big storm." Tom was already on his way. But as it turns out, Melanie was pregnant with my kid, and I didn't know it. She told me one night at dinner. Then at the same meal, she asked me, "Do you want me to have an abortion?"

Tom arrived with my business partner a few days later. We assessed the storm together to ensure I didn't miss anything of value. Then, we had a meeting of the minds. Following that meeting, we decided to go to work for the oldest and largest roofing company in Pensacola, Florida. The company had thirty-four salesmen. Within a month, we were in the number one spot in sales. Everyone needed a roof, making it so easy to sell a ton of jobs. Really, the best way to describe it was that we were order takers. Every day before five o'clock, I would sell at least three, sometimes five, roofing jobs. The money was unbelievable. The cost of roofing there was two or three times the cost of anywhere else in the country. It was as if Tom and I had unearthed our own gold mine. We even got so cocky we told customers we weren't giving estimates. We were signing contracts! We'd ask the customer to call someone else if they wanted a free estimate. Eventually, an executive from the company we worked for called me and told me I couldn't do that to people. I politely told him where to go, which was the opposite of Heaven. I told him I was cashing out all my jobs. He gave me my money, all but fourteen thousand of it.

Later I went over to inspect one of my roofing jobs. When it was finished, I signed the receipt, "Paid in full," and had the customer pay me in cash. I kept the money and told the company to consider it severance pay. While that was dishonest, by my definition of honesty today, it was just settling accounts for the unpaid commission I was owed.

## VEGAS OR BUST

But the law didn't see it that way. In the law's eyes, what I did constituted theft. I had stolen from the roofing company I worked for, and they pressed charges. After all this, I was tired of living like I was. Actually, the truth is, I had been sick and tired of being sick and tired for years. I decided to take a trip to Ohio, in order to see my parents. As I was leaving my hotel room, my phone rang. I'll never forget it; it was a warm sunny day in Pensacola, Florida. I answered my phone, and It was Melanie. She asked me what I wanted to do about the baby. I answered her as if it were just another business deal. I said, "Well, if you want to have it, you can, and if you do, you will always have financial support from me." I answered out of shock that she had called me. We were living in the same hotel, but I had seen her with other men, which hurt my pride terribly. So, out of foolish pride, I had made a fatal mistake that cost my child their life!

Approximately a month later, while I was partying in Las Vegas, Nevada. Melanie, still in Florida, boarded a plane, now determined to abort the child in her womb. She flew back to Dallas, Texas, where my ex-wife Lynn was waiting to take her to an abortion clinic to abort my child. I later learned Lynn held Melanie's hand while she had the abortion. Let me tell you something, my dear friend. As I sit here writing this book with tears in my eyes, I don't know if I will ever get over that mistake. I played a part in that abortion because I chose to possess a form of knowledge called ignorance. I chose to be selfish, self-centered, and proud. Because of that, I put Melanie in a bad spot, which cost my unborn child its life.

In retrospect, that whole period of my life taught me some very hard lessons; tragically, ones learned at the expense of another human being's life, a death I could have prevented. There isn't a word in all the languages on earth that can describe how guilty I feel when I think about my child's death. But, I thank God for his love, grace, and mercy, and most of all, for his forgiveness.

## PARTYING LIKE A ROCK STAR

"And sin, when it is full-grown, gives birth to death."

I was still on the run from charges of stealing the money I had stolen from the insurance company. I arrived in Cincinnati, Ohio, my birthplace. And now, after a very long absence, I walked into my parent's house drunk. They weren't so much surprised to see me drunk, but to see me at all. Actually, they hadn't seen me in years. So me and my old drinking buddy, my father, went down to the local bar and had some drinks. After a few, another good friend of mine named Lonnie joined us, and eventually, we called a limo and went to a party that ended up lasting for a week. Before that visit, it seemed as if I only lived to work, make a ton of money, and drink. My life had now become a self-induced torturous hell. *And over the previous dozen years or so, I had become a chemically addicted animal. I had succumbed to the disease of addiction.* During that week, my friend Lonnie and I partied and had a blast doing a lot of alcohol, drugs, and a whole harem of women. It was crazy and pitiful!

So one day, I called the same limo service and asked them to take me to the Dayton, Ohio airport, which was sixty miles away. I got there and gave my driver a two hundred dollar tip. After buying a ticket, I boarded a plane for Las Vegas, Nevada. I was carrying a lot of cash on me. Approximately five hours later, I was in Las Vegas and headed to the Mirage Casino right on the Las Vegas strip. I quickly lost thousands of dollars in six hours. But I just knew I was going to win it all back! I then made the biggest mistake you can make as a gambler. I began chasing my money like a fool. In other words, I'm still gambling and losing. But all the while, I believe I will win my money back. That mistake was not good! As it turned out, I went to Las Vegas for the weekend and stayed there for fifty-two days. I never called my family, and my brothers thought I was dead. They actually filed a missing person report. Originally, I was going to fly out to Golden Beach, Oregon on Monday, but I never did! I lost everything I had in cash, which was a lot by any person's standards.

As I drove back to my house in Texas, I realized my life was in shambles. There was something terribly wrong with me. After returning home, I worked, sold some things, begged, stole, and borrowed! But amazingly, I got back right financially, which didn't take very long. Finally, I found Melanie and married her. Wow! Can you believe that? I was definitely working on getting the most insane person of the decade award! Only kidding. We moved to a friendly neighborhood not far from my oldest brother John. And, at the outset, it seemed as though I might be on track to achieve normalcy and climb out of the pit I had been in my whole adult life. But Melanie and I fought constantly, and it was a terrible marriage. The whole time I lived in self-delusion and denial that I was the problem and that my drinking was my main problem. The power of self-deception is terrible. Looking back now, I blamed everyone and everything for my problems. What a lie. The truth was, I was the problem. But I couldn't see it at the time.

## ORGANIZED CRIME

By this time, I had been arrested multiple times for multiple assaults, multiple D.W.I.s, and drugs. What a shame. The long fall from greatness and grace had taken place, and now it is the fall of 2006. About that time, I met a guy at a bar one night; and we hit it off. The girl I was with and my new friend I had met a couple of hours earlier went back to his house. He was a connected guy with an organized crime syndicate, a made man. We got there, and I walked into a room, trying to use a bathroom. There was a printer and a dryer. I looked closer because the dryer was open, and there was a pile of something on the floor. I looked again, and I saw that it was money. I quickly walked out of the room.

We then proceeded to do some methamphetamine and started talking, and I found out that my new friend had just gotten out of prison on a thirty-year sentence. I then told him I had a brother named Brandon, who had been to prison five times. He asked me my last name, and I told him. As it turns out, right then and there, I figured out why my brother Brandon had been to prison five times. He is a member of an organized crime syndicate. *Brandon and the guy I was talking to are friends. Small world!* So I started hanging around this guy. We hit it off and then the next thing I knew we were shaking down high-level drug dealers at night while I was the general manager of a construction company during the day. I should have been admitted to a nuthouse.

By now, I'm the ripe old age of twenty-eight years old. Melanie and I have a very toxic relationship, but we have a child. She is simply beautiful and I absolutely adore her. Then one day, as I was standing there holding our daughter, Melanie said something to me, and I said something smart back to her. Then Melanie said something to the effect of, she'll take my daughter away from me in court. Next thing you know, I just reacted. I punched her in the mouth with a right jab, and I instantly realized what I had done. I started crying and apologized to her. *But the damage was done. I had knocked four of her teeth out. That is absolutely absurd. Whenever I think about that incident, I'm completely ashamed. The dental bill alone* was over five thousand dollars. That was just for the porcelain crowns. Two days later, I was arrested for domestic assault. I went to court for ten months and fought the charges valiantly. But the judge and prosecutor were very upset with me. But I must say that no one could have been more upset about that incident then I was.

# JUSTICE IS SERVED

I realized in the end that arguing my case with the prosecutor was useless because I had five prior assaults in a ten-year period. I went all the way to a jury trial, they offered a plea bargain of four years on a Friday, and the following Monday, I pleaded guilty at trial. The judge rang that gavel down. I'll never forget the words he said, "Mr. O'Dell, I find you guilty of domestic assault, and I sentence you to the Texas Department of Criminal Justice for a period of no more than seven years."

# PRISON

### "The Good Lord Is So Merciful"

It was over; I had screwed everything up and done the same to an ever-increasing list of others in their lives. The latter part of that last statement is the real shame of this tragedy. I didn't know it at the time, but God was still there through it all, even though I had just shipwrecked my life. As I sat in that cell that day and wept, I realized how hopeless my life had become. To top it all off, about a month after I was sentenced, as I watched television with another inmate, the lead news story was about a double homicide and a botched robbery of a high-level dope dealer. It was on the West Side of Ft. Worth, Texas. As I listened, I couldn't believe my ears. It was my brother's friend, the guy I was shaking down high-level dope dealers with. Apparently, he entered an apartment to rob a known drug dealer. It was my buddy, a prospect, and another guy. The prospect entered first because the people knew him. Next thing you know, the prospect started fighting with the drug dealer. After that, the guy I was running around with entered behind the prospect and immediately executed the dope dealer. There were two other people in the dope house. The guy's wife came up off the couch with a shotgun after the guy I knew fired two shots into the dope dealers buddy on the floor and looked up at the prospect; she raised the shotgun toward the prospect, and then the guy I had been running with previously, realized the prospect was gonna get shot at point-blank range with a shotgun. In a last-ditch effort to save the prospect's life, he shot the prospect down, shooting him twice in the back. As soon as the prospect was clear, the guy I knew unloaded the rest of the bullets in his magazine, killing the guy's wife. They got all the drugs and the safe full of money, and as they walked out, they realized; something was wrong! The getaway driver is gone.

The getaway driver got scared in the hail of gunfire, circled the block, and doubled back. They took the prospect to the hospital and dumped him out, as he was bleeding profusely. Turns out, the police were already on the scene of the crime, and the guy they would leave lying on the floor for dead was also rushed to the same hospital where they dumped the prospect off. Both men were rushed to surgery, and they both lived. The dope dealer's friend, who was shot and left to die, would later identify the prospect in the hospital a few weeks later. The prospect turned state's evidence. He testified in court against my acquaintance, whom I had met months earlier. *The prospect received 40 years, the primary shooter got a life sentence, and my buddy got the death penalty. How tragic. It was just pure unadulterated evil.* Do you know what the point of all this is? I would have probably been involved in that shooting. But, God, in His mercy, did not let the enemy of our souls, Satan, steal my life from me. I thank God every time I think of that tragedy. I'm grateful that God has protected me.

# CHAPTER 3

---◆◆◇◆◆---

## MY PRIVATE PRISON OF PRIDE

"The depths that the sin of pride took me to."

So now that you understand that I made, and I squandered, approximately $2,200,000 between the ripe old ages of eighteen and twenty-nine years old. I'm certain at this point, I have painted a gruesome picture for you and qualified myself as an addict, a criminal, and the epitome of selfishness. Then they slammed the door on me and gave me seven years in prison. Sadly, life was over as I knew it, and so was my eleven-year party. The inevitable finally happened and I finally went to prison. I'm certain that going to prison beats the alternative, which is death.

As soon as I got off the prison bus, fifty-four other men were with me. They stripped us down just like we came into this world. Naked! We were in a line and they made us stand so close to the other guy that we were probably just inches from him. It was very dehumanizing! They shaved all my hair off, and they made you shave all the hair off your face. You must be clean-shaven in the Texas prison system; this was the rule at the time. Shortly after your haircut and shower. A sergeant from gang intelligence comes over and looks at all your tattoos. This is to see if you're a member of a security threat group and if they can prove it. If you are, you've just earned your way to administrative segregation. This also means you'll be in a single cell. You're also probably going to do eighty-five percent of your time even if you can make parole. Finally, in administrative segregation, expect an automatic twenty-three hours-a-day lockdown. Read the book of Genesis and remember what God said. The LORD God said, "It is not good for the man to be alone. I will make a helper suitable for him" (Genesis 2:18, NIV). Especially twenty-three hours a day, in a single cell, for years!

Some of the guys that are in prison and that are in administrative segregation have life sentences. They are never getting out of prison! And that is the thing about the world; it loves conditionally, the opposite of God's love which is unconditional. The true God of Abraham, Isaac, and Jacob loves us for who we are as his beloved creation, not by what we do. In other words, God loves the sinner and hates the sin. He expects us to do the same. People ask me what is wrong with this country. That's really an easy question; we have fallen away from our first love, God. The sad part about this is that only 25% of Americans today believe that the Bible is to be taken literally. In 1970 it was 40%. That is the major problem with this country. People believe the lies of Satan instead of the word/truth of God. Let me ask you a question. Do you believe a lie? The reason why I ask that is that if you believe a lie, you choose to live a lie. The truth is what the word of God says about all of creation and your life. If you are ignorant of the Bible's truth, you automatically default to living a lie.

In the United States, we have "In God, we trust" on our money, but most people don't trust God except conditionally. We sing God Bless America, and we sing Amazing Grace on Sunday at church, yet all the while, we put God on a timetable, looking at our watches, hoping the pastor doesn't preach too long; remember, momma has a pot roast in the oven, and the Dallas Cowboys are playing at twelve o'clock. That is the main problem with America. It is our pride that is the source of all sin. Long before I ever got locked up, I had a problem with pride. The Bible says, "To respect the Lord means to hate evil. I hate pride and boasting, evil lives, and hurtful words" (Proverbs 8:13).

## PRIDE AND EGO

"Pride comes before the fall and humility before honor."

Let me tell you a little story about how foolish pride makes you look. I fought with my wife Melanie on purpose once, so I could go drinking. I was sitting at a little bar on the Southside of Ft. Worth, Texas. I'm sitting at the bar talking to this cowboy. I didn't know it then, but he was a professional saddle bronc rider. He had won twenty-eight rodeos in his lifetime before he was forced into retirement. We got drunk; imagine that! We started talking about riding bulls. Then my girlfriend Samantha comes walking up, and she is standing there listening. She is the real reason I fought with my wife, Melanie. This cowboy looked up at me and said, "I bet you that I could ride a bull longer than you can." I thought he was kidding. I said, "How much do you wanna bet?" He said, "How about five hundred dollars?".

We then shake hands and bet! We leave the bar we were at, and it is Samantha and I, my cowboy friend, and five car loads of people from this little bar that were all at partying. We make it to a town just south of Ft. Worth, Texas. It is called Crowley, Texas. We pulled up on a huge ranch. It just so happens that they retire some professional bulls at this ranch. I met with the owner, and he is a super nice guy. I looked out at the pasture, and the owner said, "Pick a bull to ride." But he quickly reminds

62

me that "I don't have to pick the biggest one!" So what do I do out of foolish pride? I picked the biggest Brahma bull out there, like an idiot. This bull has horns on him the size of Dallas, Texas! Then, the ranch hands ran the bull up into the shoot and put flank straps on it. This bull was out of control in the shoot and kicking and bucking. I go up on top of the shoot, still in dress shoes and slacks. The people there could see this was a terrible joke gone wrong. But let me tell you my thought process at the time. I never backed down from anything in my life. I was full of foolish pride, and my ego was writing checks my body couldn't cash. I would have rather died that day than back down from a challenge in front of my girlfriend, Samantha.

## RIDING FOR A FALL

Just for the record. It was a beautiful day outside, and I didn't really think this plan was a bad idea at all. I jumped on this bull, and he is so big that my legs are smashed in the shoot. They decided to double-knot the rope in my hand, not good! It was right there at that moment that I got my first clue; something was wrong! The ranch owner looked at me and said, "Son, have you ever been on a bull before?" I quickly shot back, "I did ride a few in school." He shot a sharp look at me and said, "Sign this waiver; it says, I'm not responsible if you get hurt." I looked at the two cowboys in the arena and the doorman and said, "Ok, boys. Ok, boys!" The door opened, and this bull blew out of the shoot with all four feet off the ground. I instantly tightened my legs around him as tightly as possible and braced for impact. It was brutal on my back. The bull spun to his right, he bucked, and I stayed away from his back legs and tried to keep my center of gravity up over his shoulders, watching his head for his next

63

move. Then at four seconds, I heard a familiar voice yell, "Baby!" I glanced over at the crowd in the direction of my girl, and the bull jumped straight up off the ground on all fours, bucked me off, and then I was airborne! I immediately came down face first and hit the back of the bull, almost knocking me out. The bull then spun around and stomped me on my genitals and lower leg. I quickly realized that I was in trouble, big trouble! The bull spins around, hooks me on the side, and knocks me 6 feet in the air. Right then, five cowboys came to my rescue. Fortunately, as soon as I hit the ground on the last hit, they had distracted the bull long enough for me to run. I barely made it over the shoot to safety.

After a minute, I looked at the cowboy I bet at the bar and said, "It's your turn now." And at that moment, he pulled five hundred dollars out of his wallet and said, "I'm not riding that bull!" I said, "Why not?" He said, "Because I saw what it did to you."

My friend, that was foolish pride at its best, and I woke up eight hours later urinating blood, which cost me two thousand dollars in hospital bills. Insanity! The doctor asked me, "Son, are you a professional bull rider?" I said, "No, sir." Then he told me that I could have been killed or could have busted my spleen. I didn't argue because that whole side I was hit on was now badly bruised from being hooked with the bull's horns. I just kind of laughed when the doctor told me that I could have been killed and why. A perfect analogy for my former life is what the Apostle Paul said thousands of years before I was ever even thought of, "My destiny was destruction, my God was my stomach, and my glory was in my shame" (Philippians 3:19). Sadly, that is all of humanity's destiny, if we don't make Jesus the Lord of our lives.

My philosophy in life was the world meets nobody halfway, and if I wanted something, I would have to make a way to get it. It didn't matter to me what the cost was! My ego was writing checks my body couldn't cash. I was out to make a statement to everyone and everything in life. I would prove to my earthly father and the world that I was good enough to be loved. I didn't care if I hurt myself to prove a point. I was reckless, careless, and out right foolish. That sat me up to be a very dangerous person to be around and also made me very proud, arrogant, and conceited. I had a very serious problem with pride. That is exactly what that bull ride was all about.

A man called me out in front of my girlfriend, Samantha. Then out of foolish pride, we bet, and I took a wild ride. I didn't know it at the time. But, I wish I had known then what I know now, which is that our pride is a very serious spiritual condition. Pride continually causes us to exalt ourselves above measure. Namely, the measure and stature of Christ, which is humility. It causes us to violate the word of God, by choosing not to walk humbly through this world; therefore, we don't have God's blessing upon our lives when we do this, until we correct ourselves. In other words, we are setting ourselves up as the God of our life.

In the Bible, it says, "God is against the proud, but he is kind to the humble" (1 Peter 5:5, ERV,1987). It further says, "You people are not faithful to God! You should know that loving what the world has is the same as hating God" (James 4:4). My point is that humility cures worldliness, and I loved the world in my former life. That means I defaulted to hating God, which was very proud of me. Please allow me to give you a stern warning. If you love the world, sin, and relish it. You are greatly deceived if you call yourself a Christian and live like an unbeliever.

Pride is the exaltation of one's self. Pride means that we think that we are better than anyone else. Our pride is the source of all sin. The cold hard truth is that pride is why Satan was kicked out of Heaven (Isaiah 14:13). Satan is the father of pride and lies. Pride was Adam and Eve's first sin committed in the Garden of Eden. Our Pride is the ultimate act of selfishness and self-centeredness toward God and humanity because it causes us to exalt ourselves above measure. This is why I believe that pride is the first abomination of God.

Sadly, I bought into this lie for twenty-nine years in my former life. It caused me to be selfish and self-centered, and it was the catalyst that destroyed everything in my life that made it worthwhile, which was mainly good relationships. If you looked at my life on the outside, I had it together in my career. I made a ton of money for my age, time, and education level. But inside, I was full of pride and fear because I had my faith in the things of this world instead of God through Jesus Christ. Then I added a slew of addictions and compulsions on top of my pride, ego, fear, and it almost cost me my life, because when sin is full-grown, it brings forth death. I believe that I have painted a clear enough picture so that now you can clearly see, the recipe for disaster and death that I call my former life. The saddest state that I was ever in, was the fact that at the end of my former life, it was so terrible, that I literally welcomed death.

It was fear and pride that wreaked havoc on every part of my life. It affected every aspect of my being. It was pride that caused me to build a self-imposed prison around my heart and life. Where I laid every brick of that prison myself perfectly. Every brick was made out of selfishness, self-centeredness, self-seeking, self-pity, self-delusion, and self-righteousness. My foolish pride caused me to live a life of self-propulsion and subscribe to self-will run riot. On those terms, I was always on a high-speed collision course with someone or something. It was pride that locked me inside the walls of that self-imposed prison, along with unforgiveness, and that caused me to build walls around my heart so high that you couldn't get a helicopter to fly high enough to get me out. It was pride that drove me to live in a self-induced torturous hell. It was also pride that reduced my life to a one-person and a one-cell radius. In the end, the only person left in my life was me in a prison cell. It was my foolish pride that almost killed me.

It was pride, ignorance, and poor choices that caused me to be an alcoholic and a drug addict. My pride caused me not to listen to God and those who truly loved me and to go on living a life of selfishness and self-centeredness. Then I proceeded to go on hurting myself and others. It was also my foolish pride and ignorance of God's word that caused me to shipwreck my life and make those people who loved me the most stand by and watch helplessly. Namely, my two oldest daughters, Alice and Brenda. It was pride, alcohol, and money. That caused me to walk out on my wife and children and orphan them. It was pride that caused me to make the poor choices that robbed my mother and father of fifteen years of my life because I was always locked up. It was pride, stupidity, ignorance, and foolishness on my part that emotionally extorted my mother on her deathbed, as she thought about her first born son being in a physical prison as she took her last breath.

My foolish pride robbed my three beautiful daughters of their dad and allowed me to make horrible choices that would allow another man to take care of my children. Today I live in sorrow because of that choice alone. It was pride that caused me to become a criminal, liar, cheat, thief, con, and master manipulator. It was pride and ignorance of my sin problem that cost me everything that I ever made, possessed, and loved. My good friend, I have a Ph.D. in pride. My pride caused me to take the grace of God in vain in my former life.

My pride caused me to look at the God of all creation and say, with my actions as Adam and Eve did in the Garden of Eden, "I believe in you, God. I know you're real. But you don't have the right to run my life. I will do what I want at the cost of my soul." My pride caused me to watch my fellow man walk by me to their death and say, "God, thanks for saving me. But, my faith serves me, and now that I'm saved, the rest of your creation can go straight to Hell." That is exactly what I said to the Most High God in my actions for twenty-nine years, as I continually sat myself up as the God of my life by exalting myself above measure.

In other words, I said the "sinner's prayer" when I was twelve years old. But there was no true repentance. It is absolutely horrific what foolish pride, fear, and ignorance of the word of God can do to a human being. I know a lot about pride. But there is one thing I know beyond a shadow of a doubt. Our pride is the source of all sin in humanity. It doesn't matter how you slice it. It all leads back to pride. This is why pride is the first abomination of God and the first sin ever committed by Adam and Eve.

I realize now that it is a gracious thing for God to show us the way back from our pride. Through the way of humility. It is a gracious thing for God to undermine the basis of our pride. The good Lord does this because He is rich in mercy, so we can receive his grace through the Lord Jesus Christ. God does this because He wants us to come to a "Godly sorrow that produces repentance leading to salvation, not to be regretted; but the sorrow of the world produces death" (2 Corinthians 7:10, KJV). I know a lot about the sorrow of the world.

It is absolutely insane to me today when I look back at my former life and realize the way that I acted. I thank the Lord every day that he didn't let me die in my sin, in my former life. I often think about that fateful day when I allowed my pride and ego to write a check my body couldn't cash. Needless to say, the bull humbled me that day. But, it was only for a brief moment.

# CHAPTER 4

———◆◆◇◆◆———

# INNER HEALING AND DELIVERANCE

In May of 2008, I sat in the Johnson County Jail in Cleburne, Texas. I was waiting for the Texas Department of Criminal Justice to transport me to prison. I was lying on my rack, sound asleep. It was one o'clock in the morning. I heard someone screaming at the top of their lungs, "Odell, you're on the chain; pack your stuff!" I was rudely awakened, shaken, and startled. I quickly got up, packed my stuff, and the Sheriff's Office loaded me up in the transport van, along with the four other men. We waited at the jail for about four hours in a holding cell that smelled like a sewage pipe before we were transported. We made the long drive down to Waco, Texas, at about six thirty in the morning. The town of Waco, Texas, was where Johnson County inmates went to catch the bus to prison from the Mclendon County Jail. The drive to Waco was about an hour from Cleburne, Texas, where I had been in jail for ten long months. It took the prison transport officers thirty minutes to get there to pick us all up. They called us out one by one, searched us, put shackles on our legs, and then handcuffed us. The other men and I walked down the long hallway toward the bus. The bus looked like an armored car. As I rounded the corner, a guard was standing at the rear and front of the bus with a shotgun! One of the guards shouted, "You're not in Kansas anymore." And told us in not-so-polite terms to get our butts on the bus and start sitting at the back of the bus first.

I had just turned twenty-nine years old and was now sitting in prison in East Texas, sweating half to death. The name of that prison is Joe "Butt Naked" Gurney. It was a transfer facility in Tennessee Colony, Texas. I remember it like it was yesterday. It was a hot sunny day in May, at least one hundred degrees outside. I walked out the door with the forty-seven other men in my dorm. I could feel the hot summer breeze hit my face. It was a sigh of relief! I had finally got away from the extreme heat in the dorm. It seemed as if it was hotter inside the building than it was outside. The Texas prison system has no air conditioning anywhere inmates live unless it is a medical unit. A lot of the buildings are 26 gauge steel R-Panel. The metal that the building is made out of, heats up during the summertime, and the heat transfers perfectly through the walls. I can only think of one word to describe that, horrible! I had only been in prison for a couple of days. The county jail I came from had air conditioning, making it twice as hard to adjust to the heat. Ideally, I would go to prison in the winter and gradually get used to the summer heat. On this particular day there was a lot of inmates that was moving up and down the strip to get to the cafeteria and back to the dormitory while my cellmates and I were walking there to eat. The guards were standing there calling people out of the line who they thought looked suspicious. They would strip search you right there on the spot in front of about a hundred inmates, and there are always at least two or three women guards. I hated getting stripped out in front of a woman. But, as fate would have it. I made a mistake on this particular day and looked at a rookie officer. Academy officers are taught to assume that if an inmate cuts their eyes at them, he is probably muling something back from the cafeteria. It was usually stolen food. So this guard decided to pull me over. He looked at me and said, "Hey, inmate come here." I never looked at him because if he didn't want me and I looked, I just bought myself a strip search. Make no mistake, my friend, if it is twenty-five degrees outside, you still get stripped and searched. If you were like me and liked to be a smart mouth, call the guards homosexuals and a few other choice words, which they weren't—they were just doing their job—you would stand out there for twenty minutes, naked as a newborn baby. Then much to my surprise, the Warden, a woman, walked out of the officers' dining room. She looked right at her officers and said, "This is starting to look like a nudist colony." I look to my right and see two of my homeboys getting searched. I think to myself, those guys look pathetic. I remember also thinking at the exact same time, I will bet anything that I look just like those poor pathetic losers! While standing there, I drifted off to the free world, where nothing is free. I was suddenly there with my second wife, Melanie, and my youngest daughter. My daughter was born on August 28, 2007, and I got locked up on September 4, 2007. Finally, the guard yells, "Get your clothes on, inmate, and go back to the dorm; dinner is over."

## A SERIOUS WAKE-UP CALL

I remember getting back to the dorm and as soon as I stepped through the door. It was as if somebody had just put a warm wet blanket around me. The heat was miserable. I remember sitting on my bunk looking out at the guys in the day room. Guys were gambling in one corner, smoking cigarettes in another, and people were cooking food, just having a wonderful time. I remember thinking, "You really did it this time." It was finally getting real, and I can specifically remember this feeling of dread coming over me.

My life was over as I had known it, at least temporarily! I remember thinking what is wrong with me? I looked over, and a few inmates were talking about God in a corner. One of them yelled out, "Prayer call." As I heard that, something deep down inside of me nudged at me, kind of like a cat nudges you when he wants you to pet him. I needed to go over there. I needed something positive in my life at that moment. So, I went to the prayer call, and we talked about God. We then prayed and shook hands. I slept like a baby that night.

I woke up and as I looked around the dorm. I could remember thinking to myself, wow! I thought to myself again. What went wrong? What is wrong with me, that I was willing to reduce myself to such a meager existence? I got in my locker to get a toothbrush to brush my teeth, and low and behold, there was my Bible. I didn't really read the Bible per se. I just used it to store my phone numbers. The good thing for me was on this particular day that I'm talking about, I was all out of options. I was also bored, so I decided to read the Bible. It made me feel a lot better. Just to let you know where I was at mentally and emotionally, I was really an absolute mess. I remember looking across the dayroom and the television show "Good Morning America" was on the television. The sunlight was barely coming in the small windows. As I looked up and started watching the show, there was a mother holding a newborn baby on the television. It was almost as if Mike Tyson had hit me with a body blow right in the stomach. I wanted to cry, and tears even came to my eyes as I thought about my youngest daughter. She had just been born ten months earlier. I thought about how I chose to make a ton of bad decisions and how I orphaned her to come to prison. I remember feeling helpless and hopeless. One thing was for certain, though! Rule number one is that you never show emotion in prison. It is taken as a sign of weakness. Which, by the way, is not even human. Another problem I had, as I look back now, was that I had to answer to my homeboys. They would have disciplined me for crying. Make no mistake, inside and outside, my world was coming to an end. I hurt so bad on the inside at this point in my life that you could see my internal problems externally now. In other words, instead of living in a self-imposed prison, I also lived in a physical prison! In retrospect, I realize now that I lived in the pure and perfect bondage of self. The only thing I could do was continue to push my feelings down and not show any emotions. I started working out two hours a day. I was going to make my body a weapon of mass destruction. This helped relieve a lot of stress at the time. It helped channel some of my negative energy in a positive direction. But, in the end, I became a violent criminal. The main reason for this was that I had to answer to my homeboys. But, the prison I was housed at was full of violent people.

## HURTING PEOPLE WILL HURT OTHERS

The main reason I became so violent was that my hurts, pain, and emotions had nowhere to go and no way to be expressed. This scenario kept playing over and over in my head. I kept having self-defeating thoughts like I was a terrible father, that I was a terrible husband, that I was a terrible person. As far back as I can remember, I never had a chance not to become a statistic. One of the main problems of being incarcerated was that the guards were always yelling and screaming at us all the time. I was so angry that I woke up every day wondering who's head am I going to knock off today? I became a very angry young man. Looking back, I should have talked to a chaplain or someone. But, as fate would have it. That was way too human

74

for a guy like me at the time. I became an animal. I mean, my line of thinking was that I lived at the zoo and was one of the animals. It was a dog-eat-dog world, and there was one thing for sure. I was not going down without a fight! A few months earlier, I was eating at the finest steakhouse in Ft. Worth, Texas, and then all of a sudden, I was eating slop, living with killers, rapists, and thieves. Wow! What a turn of events.

I was constantly reading the Bible and that did help me a lot mentally. But the only problem was that I wasn't a doer of God's word. I want you to understand something that I didn't at the time. If all else fails, you have to be a hearer and doer of God's word. The Bible says, "Those who hear God's teaching and do nothing are like people who look in a mirror. They see their faces and then go away quickly and forget what they looked like. But the truly happy people are those who carefully study God's perfect law that makes people free, and they continue to study it. They do not forget what they heard, but they obey what God's teaching says. Those who do this will be happy" (James 1:23-25). I didn't know any of this at the time. But, as I glance back at my former life. I can see that the good Lord was always right there with me. Prison life was terrible, and the meal of the day was racism, prejudice, anger, hatred, and bitterness! *Looking back now, the most insane part of prison was when we sat in the day room of prison and sensationalized drugs and crime.* In other words, we were so terribly deceived, and our whole life had become a lie. But these guys and I were making plans to come back to prison before we had ever got out. We were like sheep heading to the slaughter and didn't even know it.

# BECOMING A BOOKIE

Sadly, my whole life was nothing more than an evil, insidious lie. I was sick and tired of being sick and tired. My world was coming to an end, and as fate would have it, my second wife, Melanie, went absent without orders to leave at the time. Shortly after she quit writing to me, I got served with divorce papers. At the time, I blamed her. Of course, I know better now, and as I look back now, I know and believe that it wasn't her fault. I abandoned her and my daughter to go to prison for seven years, and it was because of my poor choices. I was saddened by the turn of events, but I moved on. After about a year and being denied parole two times, I suddenly realized I was in prison for the long haul and that the Texas Board of Pardons and Parole was not going to give me parole. I finally ran out of the money I desperately needed to buy hygiene products that the prison sold from the commissary we were allowed to go to once a week.

My homeboy owned a bookie operation. They had people running it for them all over the whole prison compound. I really needed money, so I found a way to make it. I took a job running a bookie operation for the dorm that I stayed in. Everyone likes to gamble in prison. I knew it was the perfect scam. Shortly after this, I learned the intricacies of the day-to-day operations in the sports booking business. Then I ran the operation for the building I was housed in. About three months later, I began running the operation for the building I was housed in. I was asked to run the whole operation for the compound. I gladly accepted the offer. It wasn't until then that I realized how much money was really in the sports booking business. On any given weekend for the whole prison compound, we would take in approximately $700.00. We would pay out about two hundred of that. Sometimes a little more. We made roughly $2,000 a month in profit. We paid each guy in each dorm around the prison compound a percentage for taking the tickets. The crazy part about this is that if we had gotten caught running a sports booking operation, it would have been an automatic one-year set off on our parole. In other words, we would have automatically stayed in prison for one more year on our sentence. The sports booking operation had about 30 homeboys involved, not counting all the other people like the dorm janitors and outside clean-up guys. We employed them to get those tickets to us before the games started. We were masterminds! One thing about it, nobody was gonna scam the scammers. The sports booking business is tough. You practically have to eat, sleep, and breathe sports. One wrong move, and you can lose hundreds of dollars on a ticket the customer might only have $5 on! It was stressful. We would call into Vegas on Tuesday when the lines came out. We would get the lines from five different casinos. Then we would call back on Thursday and get the late lines, so to speak. We would be gambling from prison ourselves through a third party. I got to be so good at doing the numbers that I would make my own lines, and ironically, my lines would work better than the Las Vegas, Nevada lines a lot of times.

The whole time I was doing the sports booking operation, I was reading the Bible for about an hour and a half a day. But the word of God was null and voided in my life. The reason I wasn't walking in victory is very simple; I was paying God lip service, and I was not continuing to work out my salvation with fear and trembling. I was a hearer of God's word and not a doer. The Bible says, "But be doers of the word, and not hearers only, deceiving yourselves. But be sure you live out the message and do not merely listen to it and so deceive yourselves" (James 1:22). I was still full of the same pride that got me to prison in the first place. In effect, I was still telling God, "I believe in you, Lord, but you don't have the right to run my life." I was basically telling my Creator that I knew what was best for my life. That is very foolish and prideful! Remember, "Pride goes before destruction, and haughty spirit before a fall" (Proverbs 16:18, ERV). I went to church in prison every Saturday. But the only problem was that it wasn't to worship God. Church in prison is where all the gangs meet and discuss business. Although it was intended for evil, the good thing was that it seemed like no matter what was going on in church, and even though I was there for all the wrong reasons, I could always hear the preacher. It felt like something was being stirred inside of me.

I believed in God, but so do the demons, and they tremble at the fact! The real question was, did I believe God enough to love him in truth and action? Did I continue to believe, repent, and work out my salvation with fear and trembling on a daily basis? The answer is a very sharp no. I liked playing the god of my life and playing with God. But God is so merciful, and I believe He knew I was searching for him. God is so gracious and patient. God kept calling me back through the way of humility. The Lord kept shocking me into an awareness of my helplessness, through the way of humility, into his amazing saving grace. Somewhere deep down inside was the real James Odell. The son of James and Emma Bolton. The good son, father, fellow, and husband. But Satan, the god of this world, had crippled me spiritually when I was young. Satan had robbed me of my identity in Christ because if you don't know your identity in Christ, then you don't know who you are in Christ, or your eternal value. If you don't understand your eternal value. Then you can't understand how much God loves you. If you can't understand how much God loves you and why. There is no way you can understand the cross and the gospel of Jesus Christ. Therefore you can't bow to the one and only true God. No doubt, you can never understand why Jesus died on the cross. The Bible says, "We are his workmanship created in Christ Jesus to do good works which he prepared for us in advance" (Ephesians 2:10). We are a masterpiece in God's eye. God broke the mold when he made each of us. There is nobody else on earth that has our D.N.A. We are the apple of God's eyes. He has every hair on our head counted. He is a personal God, the one matters to him, and God proved this on the cross!

Every life is a story, and every single last story matters. What I didn't know at the time was that if I had been the only one to sin and fall short of the glory of God, then God would have still sent his son Jesus Christ to die, just for me. My only problem was that I didn't know this at the time. I realize now that I was still playing the god of my life. The sin of pride is a terrible thing, and I was greatly deceived. What I needed was inner healing deliverance from all the pain in my heart. I was mortally wounded in my heart when I walked out on my ex-wife Suzanne and two oldest daughters Alice and Brenda that fateful day. There is no doubt as I look back on my life that it was because my father did not validate that he loved me. It was this fact that had sent my life into an unrecoverable tailspin. It was as if I was a pilot, and I knew my plane was hit, but I refused to press the eject button. I never realized this at the time because of everything that was going on in my life. I was going down in a blaze of glory. I know now that we are as sick as the secrets we keep. I had a ton of secrets that I needed someone I could trust to show me how to let them go. But I was too proud to ask for help.

# IDENTITY COMES THROUGH CHRIST

As I sat in West Texas, at a level 5 maximum security unit. I was broken, full of pain, and terribly misunderstood. I didn't realize it at the time, but to get inner healing and deliverance, you have to find faith. It is very funny how life works out. There are two things that drive a man, and that is fear or faith! What had happened to me is Satan, the god of this world, had robbed me of my identity as a person by keeping me ignorant of the truth and the living word, which is Jesus Christ. Jesus said, "I am the way, the truth, and the life" (John 14:6). The second truth is the gospel truth. The Bible says, "*In view of God's mercy, offer your bodies as a living sacrifice, for this is your spiritual act of worship. Do not conform any longer to the patterns of this world. But be transformed by the renewing of your mind through the word of God. Then you will be able to know the acceptable, holy, pleasing, perfect will of God" (Romans 12:1-2).* The third truth was the power of God's Holy Spirit of Truth. I wish I knew then what I know now: Satan preys on our ignorance. In other words, our lack of the knowledge of the truth of the word of God. I was terribly deceived. But because I chose to be ignorant of the word of God. I had no faith. The Bible says, "Faith comes by hearing, and by hearing the word of God" (Romans 10:17). Without faith, you have no hope! The Bible says, "Faith is the substance of things hoped for, and evidence of things not yet seen" (Hebrews 11:1). You might have temporary, conditional hope in yourself, people, places, and things. But you do not have a living hope from the one and only true God. I realize now that hope outside of God is true hopelessness. That is the absolute truth. In my former life, I had fallen for the oldest trick in the book from the enemy of my soul. I believed there was hope outside of Jesus Christ. I put my hope in money, women, people, places, and things. The sad truth is, that me having my hope in all the wrong places, caused me to live a life that was doomed to a slow, painful, death. Where I was always on a collision course with someone or something. I had put my faith in my fear. Faith leads, and fear drives. *I put my faith in money for a fear of being poor. I put my faith in people because I wanted to be loved and accepted. I had a fear of not being approved by others. I put my faith in king alcohol because I feared reality.* Bill Wilson, the founder of Alcoholics Anonymous, said in the A.A. big book, "Selfishness and self-centeredness were the roots of all our troubles. We were driven by a hundred forms of fear, self-delusion, self-seeking, and self-pity. We stepped on the toes of our fellows, and they always retaliated. Sometimes seemingly without provocation, but we have found if we searched long and hard enough, we played a part." I definitely played the part through self-will running rampant.

Fear had driven me to the gates of a living hell, where I placed myself beyond the point of human aid. *Where only my willingness to be rigorously honest and open-minded to the fact that a power greater then myself could love me back from a self-induced torturous hell, where I had become a chemically addicted animal.* Where everything in life that made it worthwhile became non-existent, I was emotionally detached from relationships. They were all gone, and it was sad. There I was, Almighty God's creation. I was made in his image. In other words, I was a relational being. But, I believed I only needed money. I was greatly deceived! I lived in total darkness like I had never known before. There was not one good relationship in my life at this point. I come to know utter hopelessness and despair like few human beings ever experience or come back from.

*That is why I'm writing this book with tears rolling down my cheeks. You see, my good friend. These tears are not for me! They're for the addict who still lives in active addiction. They're for the man or woman that made a few mistakes that sits in a physical prison but has lived in the prison they built around their heart for years.* They live in a prison that they cry to escape but don't know how. These tears are for the addicts who walked out of the Hancock County Jail and lost the fight against addiction. Their memory is forever etched in my mind. That is who these tears really belong to. One girl, as she walked out, I looked at her and said, "Take care of yourself." She politely looked back and said, "You too, O'Dell." Approximately five hours later, she was dead on arrival at the hospital from a Fentanyl overdose! Sadly, her one-year-old son was orphaned. The poor kid is left behind, wondering what his mom was like. That is terrible. I know that at the end of the road of self-sufficiency, God gives you a choice to live or die. The Bible says, "Today I have given you a choice between life and death, success and disaster" (Deuteronomy 30:15). I encourage you to read all of Deuteronomy 30 of the Bible.

## UTTER HOPELESSNESS

My day to die was near. I was already as dead as a man in the grave anyways. I didn't even feel human any more. It was a very sad time in my life. I needed a spiritual experience. I needed more faith, and I needed true hope. I didn't know it at the time, but you have no hope without faith. I kept reading the Bible, although I was never a doer of God's word.

I continued to play the god of my life and those around me. Looking back now, it was all out of foolish pride and ignorance of the scriptures. I had a rebellious spirit. At the rate I was going, I would never be a doer of God's word. But the good thing was I enjoyed reading it. That definitely helped me to some degree. The only problem was that I couldn't walk in victory since I wasn't a doer of God's word.

It was then things took a turn for the worse. I was making my ascent to the top of the criminal underworld. I became a shot caller in the Texas prison system. I subscribed to an ideology that was full of hatred and bitterness. One of the main reasons is that I had so much unforgiveness in my heart toward myself and others for what I had done and become; I hated my life and myself. The Bible says, "If you forgive others for their sins, your father in heaven will also forgive you for your sins. But if you don't forgive others, your father in heaven will not forgive your sins" (Matthew 6:14-15). *Please read this carefully. Unforgiveness is sin unto death! When you choose to allow the spirit of unforgiveness in your heart. Six other spirits follow it. That is bitterness, retaliation, anger, hatred, violence, and murder.* That is exactly why God tells you to forgive.

Also, the two greatest commandments in the Scriptures are, "Love the Lord your God with all your heart and with all your soul and with all your mind and with all your strength.' The second is this: "Love your neighbor as yourself. There is no commandment greater than these" (Mark 12: 29-31). The Bible also said, "Love does not carry a record of wrongs" (1st Corinthians 13:5). In other words, what that verse means is love is not bitter. If you choose not to forgive yourself or others. You are very proud to think God forgave you for all your sins you have ever committed in the past, present, and future. But you can't forgive your neighbor for his or her trespasses. When you choose to harbor unforgiveness in your heart, this gives the devil a foothold. Then you have not only violated the two greatest commandments in the Bible, but also the forgive, or you will not be forgiven scripture (Matthew 6:14). This scripture includes forgiving yourself also.

The Bible says, "Above all else, guard your heart, for everything you do flows from it" (Proverbs 4:23). I had a serious heart condition called a sin problem. I had a Spiritual Malady, and the road to nowhere definitely led to me. I kept reading the Bible and praying it was helping me. It was starting to take root in my heart. I needed faith, "Which comes by hearing the word of God" (Romans 10:17). A faith meaning the substance of things hoped for (Hebrews 11:1).

## THE LOVE OF THE FATHER

But sadly, no matter what happened. I still had a major problem. I needed to feel loved, needed, and wanted. The Bible says, "So these three things remain forever: Faith, hope, and love. And the greatest of these is love" (1st Corinthians 13:13). I want to crystallize this in your mind right now. The Bible also said, "I may give away everything I have, and I may even give my body as an offering to be burned. But I gain nothing if I do not have love" (1 Corinthians 13:3).

You see my good friend, the Bible says, "God is love" (1 John 4:8). So in effect, what the Bible is saying is that if you want to know how to truly love, you must go to the author of love, Almighty God. Then you can understand that the love of God is unconditional. Unlike the love of the god of this world, at the complete opposite end of the spectrum. Satan always sells humanity conditional love. Satan always distorts the truth.

The Bible says, "Love is patient and kind. Love is not jealous, does not brag, and is not proud. Love is not rude, is not selfish, and does not get upset with others. Love carries no record of wrongs. Love is not happy with evil but is happy with the truth. Love patiently accepts all things. It always trusts, hopes, and always remains strong. Love never fails" (1Corinthians 13:4-8). The reason love never fails is that God is love. It is impossible for God to fail!

God puts a void in all of our hearts. It's like an internal compass. It is made to guide us into a relationship with our Creator. God reserves the right to fill that void in all of our hearts. I tried to fill it with all the false comforters that the god of this world, Satan, had to offer. But nothing in all of creation could fill that void, I assure you! The reason is that the God of all comfort reserves the right to fill the void in our hearts.

The God of love, grace, mercy, power, wisdom, and justice is what I needed. That is what I was really searching for. I was tired of fighting. I was sick and tired of being sick and tired! One of my main problems was that I didn't know how to surrender my life to the Lord. I had fought everyone and everything for so long and so hard that fighting was all I had ever known. I thrived on the chaos. I wanted peace, but when I got peace, it was temporary. The main reason why was because usually it came from alcohol, drugs, sex, or a stack of one hundred dollar bills.

I was taught that old saying by Winston Churchill when Adolf Hitler was mounting his attack on London, England, way back in 1941, at the Harrow Boarding School that he attended in 1888. He spoke these eight words: "Never give up, never, never, never give up!" My former life was the epitome of those words. I was taught to fight on to the bitter end. That a man makes his own way! That's the human spirit! Please allow me to tell you that is a lie from the pits of Hell. That is from the author of lies, Satan himself! He knew what I didn't. The truth was, selfishness and self-centeredness were the root of sin, pride is the source of all sin, and they run hand in hand. Satan also knew that my free-will is what my problem was in the first place. Sadly, unless I surrendered my God-given free will, every single detail of my life, and bowed to the one and only true God of everything in all creation. I was doomed, and so was all of humanity!

Unless I admitted to God that I accepted Jesus Christ as my savior and allowed Jehovah to be the God of my life, I would remain hopeless forever and be lost for eternity. The end was near, and I welcomed death wholeheartedly. I had been led by the enemy of my soul like a sheep to the slaughter. I couldn't let go of the past. Although I wanted to, I didn't know how. I loved playing the god of my life and those around me! Sadly, I was pitiful at it. My whole life had become an evil, insidious lie. I realize I wasn't made to be the God of my life, anyone, or anything. I was anointed to be James Odell. The son of James and Emma Bolton. For the first time in my life, I'm actually proud of that fact. I also realize now that I am a son of God. At that point in my former life, I realized something was terribly wrong with me. I just didn't know what to do or the solution to my problems. What would I do? I would do what any man with foolish pride would do. I would press toward the mark of greatness. Sadly, me pressing towards the mark of greatness by my own strength and God-given free will were the problems that got me into the mess I was in. In other words, I was still choosing to be a part of the problem, instead of the solution. I ended up doing two months shy of five years on that seven-year sentence. I should have been home in seven to fourteen months. The whole messed up part about this is that my children were growing up fatherless the whole time I was in and out of prison.

But make no mistake! God, who is rich in mercy, had a plan. Although I stayed in prison for five years, I read the Bible for five years and made progress by God's grace. The only question was, would I truly repent? I often wondered how God could forgive me for all I had done to people. That was the main question on my mind. As a twelve-year-old boy, I had said the "sinner's prayer" on August 17, 1991. I was saved, right? Wrong! The reason is that saying the "sinner's prayer" is only regretting that you're a sinner; it must be followed with true repentance. The question was not if I repented. But if I would continue to repent and believe one day at a time and live by the narrow way of the Bible. If our faith is not perfected by our works, then that is a lack of faith demonstrated. What was amazing to me, from the age of twelve until I was forty-one years old, I called myself a Christian, which by the way, means to be Christ-like. Then after saying the "sinner's prayer," I thought I had repented. But, I confused repentance with regretting that I was a sinner. I realize now that salvation is by faith and faith alone in Jesus Christ and must be preceded and followed by true repentance. In other words, a turning away from sin and loving what God loves. Also, I must hate what God hates, and God hates sin.

## THE DREAM

This is the story on why I said the "Sinner's Prayer".As I woke up one August morning in the Texas hill country and stepped out of my room. The Texas heat was already blistering hot at nine o' clock in the morning. I looked up at the hills all around the boys' ranch. It was a beautiful, sunny day in Burnet, Texas. The sunlight was so bright it would make your eyes hurt. The night before, I had a very weird dream. There was a battle of good and evil in my room. It wasn't an ordinary dream. This dream was very real and different from any other dream I have ever had. It was as if I had stepped outside of my body. I was then attacked by a presence that I could not see. But I could sense the presence of pure unadulterated evil. The force quickly subdued me on the floor. The harder I fought, the more I realized that resistance was futile.

I cried out to God and said, "God help me!" There was no response. Then I started to feel like I was being suffocated. I cried out again, "God help me!" This time there was another presence I could sense but not see. That presence began to take over the presence that had subdued me. It was so real when I woke up on the floor. I was gasping for air. I was asleep in my bed initially. I have never to this day had a dream as real as that one in the early morning hours of August 17, 1991!

I was scared when I woke up that morning. I found myself wondering what the dream meant. I thought about my life and where it was going. I had been to church and didn't want to burn in Hell. I really wanted the blessings and prosperity that I had heard Christian people talk about. Who doesn't? I grew up poor and said to myself, "I'll take a mansion in the sky. You know what? I'll take two of them." My point is that I didn't understand what I was doing and the process of salvation, sanctification, and transformation. The Bible says, "Therefore, my beloved, as ye have always obeyed, not only in my presence but now much more in my absence, work out your own salvation with fear and trembling" (Philippians 2:12). Looking back now, I realize that I didn't continue to work out my salvation with fear and trembling.

There is no doubt in my mind today that what I did was regret that I was a sinner. Sadly, regret is one step toward repentance. But to repent, you must continue to turn away from sin with the right motive of the heart. In other words, when I repented, it should have been because God was worthy of the glory, honor, and praise in my life and all of creation. It is not about me going to Heaven or Hell. It is definitely not about me getting anything. But, it is about me surrendering my God-given free will and every single detail of my life back to God. The motive of my heart is that God is worthy. At twelve years old, I didn't have the right motive in my heart. The Bible says, "Do not consider his appearance or his height, for I have rejected him. The Lord does not look at the things people look at. People look at the outward appearance, but the Lord looks at the heart" (1 Samuel 16:7, NIV). I hung up the phone with the God of the universe that day in August of 1991 and went A.W.O.L., serving myself and Satan's purposes from twelve to forty-one years old. All the while, I believed I was a Christian. Also, while I told others I was a Christian. The crazy thing about this was that I immediately reverted to my old behavior. I also exhibited no fruits of the spirit. There was no faith being perfected by my works. In other words, my faith was dead like the Bible says, "You foolish person! Must you be shown that faith that does nothing is worth nothing" (James 2:20, ERV)? One thing about it is, that God can't lie. The Bible says, "For it is by grace you have been saved, through faith—and this is not from yourselves, it is the gift of God—not by works, so that no one can boast" (Ephesians 2:8-9). There were no fruits of the spirit in my life. That generally is a first sign indicator that your profession of faith is a sham.

# SPIRITUAL MALADY = SIN PROBLEM

What I needed was inner healing from all my hurts and pain. I also needed deliverance from sin, sickness, disease, and death, but mainly the sin in my life. "We all have sinned and fallen short of the glory of God" (Romans 3:23). My sin problem had become so bad that it nearly drove me crazy trying to fight it on my own accord. It is useless to fight sin with your own free will. Our God-given free will is what got all of humanity into this mess in the first place, ever since the fall of mankind in the Garden of Eden. The Bible says, "Wisdom is the principal thing; therefore get wisdom: and with all thy getting get understanding" (Proverbs 4:7, KJV). In order to solve my sin problem. I would have to identify the problem first, and then I would have to be honest enough to admit I had a problem. After the first two steps, I would have to treat the problem at its root cause. Treating the symptoms of my sin problem wouldn't be the answer. The facts of the matter was that I had been told my entire life that I had a problem with alcohol, and a problem with this or that. But these are facts! These are symptoms of a more deeply rooted problem. My real problem was what the Bible says, "We know that the law is spiritual, but I am not spiritual since sin rules me as if I were its slave. I do not understand the things I do. I do not do what I want to do, and I do the things I hate. And if I do not want to do the hated things I do, that means I agree that the law is good. But I am not really the one doing these hated things; it is sin living in me that does them. Yes, I know that nothing good lives in me—I mean, nothing good lives in the part of me that is earthly and sinful. I want to do the things that are good, but I do not do them. I do not do the good things I want to do, but I do the bad things I do not want to do. So if I do things I do not want to do, then I am not the one doing them. It is sin living in me that does those things" (Romans 7:14-20). That was the root cause of all my troubles. I had a sin problem that would kill me if it was left unchecked by Jesus Christ. I had to treat my sin problem with Jesus. I learned what the Bible says about sin, "The wages of sin is death, but the free gift of God is eternal life through Christ Jesus our Lord" (Romans 6:23).

Sadly, I would not take the treatment for my sin problem. It took me until I was 41 years old to figure out what you just learned in five minutes. If I had known that passage from the Bible in my former life, I would have accepted it and applied it to my life. It probably would have saved countless other people and me a lot of time and trouble. I chose to possess a form of knowledge about the Bible called ignorance, which means a lack of knowledge of the truth. The Bible is the absolute truth! The Bible is God's final answer for all of creation's problems. That law in Romans 7:14-20 the Apostle Paul is talking about is called the curse of the law of sin and death. It was passed on to all of humanity because of what Adam and Eve did in the Garden of Eden. The law is the same every time. You can defy a law with another law, but the original law is still active, like the law of gravity. When you fill a hot air balloon with helium, the law of gravity is still there, but another law supersedes it. It is called the law of buoyancy. So the higher law takes effect. That is exactly what is happening to us. We're born spiritually dead from a generational curse passed down to us by Adam and Eve. Eve means the mother of all living. The curse of the law of sin and death is upon us because of what Adam and Eve did in the garden.

When we accept the one-time ransom sacrifice that God provides for us, by confessing with our mouth that Jesus Christ is Lord and believing in our heart that God raised him from the dead, we are saved by grace through our faith in Jesus Christ. It is not by works, lest any man should boast. In other words, we surrender our God-given free will, which got us all into this spiritual malady. Then we surrender every detail of our lives to God. We do this with the right motive of our heart, being that God is the Creator and Sustainer of everything in all of existence and therefore is worthy of the glory, honor, and praise in our lives. After this fact, as the Bible talks about, we must continue to work out our salvation with fear and trembling. Then we will see the fruits of the Spirit develop in our lives to God's glory. We will also, by this time, know what it means to have to die to ourselves one moment at a time, one day at a time. Then our faith can be perfected by our works. The Bible says, "It is not I who lives, but Christ who lives in me, the life I live, I live by faith in the son of God. Because he loved and gave himself for me" (Galatians 2:20). You see my brother or sister, when I died to myself and got me out of the way and did these things, it was then and only then, that God's Holy Spirit could be exalted in my body. Then God could show me how to love myself and others.

The Bible says, "For it is God which worketh in you both to will and to do for his good pleasure" (Philippians 2:13, NKJV). When we surrender, we allow God to love and help people through us. Remember these words as long as you live. The Bible says, "Not by might nor by power, but by my spirit," saith the Lord host (Zechariah 4:6, NKJV). Remember how I just told you about one law superseding another? The Bible also says, "Through Christ Jesus, the law of the Spirit that brings life, made me free from the law that brings sin and death" (Romans 8:2). Praise the Lord God. Did you read what that verse says? In effect, it says true freedom from our sin problem, which separates us from God, comes from Jesus Christ. Listen to these words. The truth shall set you free. Jesus said, "I am the way, the truth, the life, and no man shall cometh to the Father but by me" (John 14:6). Let me ask you a question. Have you ever heard someone call the Bible the gospel truth? That is another one of the three truths that set us free. The Bible says, "Therefore, I urge you brothers, in view of God's mercy, offer your body as a living sacrifice, holy and pleasing to God. This is your spiritual act of worship. Do not conform any longer to the patterns of this world. But be transformed by the renewing of your mind through the word of God. Then you will know the acceptable, holy, pleasing, and perfect will of God" (Romans 12:1-2, NIV). Three truths give us true freedom. These three truths are Jesus, the Holy Spirit of Truth, and the Bible. When you live by these three truths, nothing in all of creation can stop you from glorifying God with your life. These three truths are what I needed to know back then. But sadly, I would fight on to the bitter end like a fool.

## TIME SERVED AND ANOTHER CHANCE AT LIFE

I got out of prison for the first time in May 2012. I received another chance at life! I remember it like it was yesterday. It was another hot summer day in Texas. I was leaving prison after fifty-eight months and finally going home. However, it was approximately eleven in the morning. It was extremely hot outside that day. I walked out of prison from the Walls unit in

Huntsville, Texas. That is also where they execute death row inmates. In all, 50 other inmates and I walked out of the East Side of the Walls Unit. As soon as we rounded the corner, people's loved ones were waiting for them. Some of them cried and were happy to get their family members back. Some of us took a walk over to the store. We cashed our checks and then bought cigarettes and beer. I just bought cigarettes on this particular day. I remember thinking to myself that day. I wished I had someone that loved me enough to come down here and welcome me back to the free world. I said to myself, "Yea, right, get real. Nobody cares if you live or die." I walked to the bus station one building away from the store and boarded a bus for Tyler, Texas. I was heading to a place called Calvary Commission. It is known as Calvary International Bible Institute and Theological Seminary today. It was the hardest thing I had ever done. The reason why was that I had gone to prison five years earlier when my youngest daughter was a newborn baby. A lot of time passed, and I hadn't seen her. At that time, she was almost five years old, and I wanted to go home and see her.

My only problem was the fact that I was on parole for twenty-six months. Also, I had been paroled to that address, so I had to appear at the parole office at nine in the morning in Tyler, Texas. It was awful when we arrived in Dallas, Texas. The distance between my daughter and me was approximately fifteen miles. I had not seen her in five years. It was very difficult, and I wanted to go home, but I couldn't. As I looked over, I saw a woman with a phone, and the phone looked very weird to me. When I went to prison, they had flip phones; five years later, when I got out of prison, they had touch screen phones. It was almost like I had been stuck in a time capsule and the world moved on without me. I started praying that God would give me a sign that I was doing the right thing. When I got done praying, I heard God say, "Be still and know that I am God." I had been praying and reading the Bible the whole time I was in prison. But now I'm hearing from God through his spirit, which is in me acting according to his will and good purpose. But, I hadn't learned to yield to his spirit and be obedient to him yet. But I'm hearing from him, and I recognize it as God. I didn't realize this then, but I was making progress. I then arrived at Calvary Commission. I got settled in, then walked down the stairs to the restroom. I turned to wash my hands, and I almost fell over dead. You wouldn't believe this in a million years! A sign on the wall said, "Be still and know that I am God." Do you think that is a coincidence? Let me give you a very sharp no on that last question. But perhaps the sign is what I call a fingerprint of God on my life back then. It was almost like God was saying to me, "My hand is guiding you, son." I couldn't believe it. I was shocked!

Well, I lasted thirty days at the school and then high-tailed it back to Arlington, Texas. My daughter and ex-wife Melanie were staying there at the time. One of the main reasons I used to justify my leaving the school was that I owed $1,380.00 a month child support. It was a stipulation of my parole that I make monthly payments to the Attorney General's Office, or they would immediately violate my parole and send me back to prison. I quickly settled back into the free world, only to realize that nothing is free in this world. I realized that my spiritual freedom was paid for by the blood of God's son. But, the physical freedom I had taken for granted was paid for with the loss of the lives of American soldiers, mostly on foreign soil! I was grateful to be out of prison.

# A MAJOR COME BACK

Yep, I was starting to see the light. But I had some serious issues to deal with. I was addicted to alcohol, women, and money. So as fate would have it, I ended up taking a job with a roofing company out of Crowley, Texas. I went over to interview for the job of General Manager, and of course, thirty minutes later, I took control and command of the company, answering only to the owner. I was going back to tell my girlfriend Becky I was going to Temple, Texas, to chase a hail storm that had just occurred. I was ready to make the big money I was used to making. I ran down a checklist of everything I needed personally and business-wise. I did exactly how I was taught fourteen years earlier. The phone rang, and I almost jumped through the ceiling of the truck. It was my secretary at the corporate headquarters. She quickly said, "Jerry wants you to stay in town tonight. Don't go to Temple. There's a hail storm that just pounded Mineral Wells, Texas, with four-inch hail." Jerry was my new boss and the owner of the company.

Cha ching, all I saw were dollar signs. Years earlier, I had made millions in a decade, and so I decided right then in there, that I would try to make millions of dollars a year. I drove to Mineral Wells, Texas, the very next day. It was like a war zone, and it was made of money. I quickly got on twelve roofs that day. I sold one job on the very first day. I was all over that hail storm, and it was like I had never missed a beat—even though I had been absent from the roofing industry for five years. I knocked them dead, and I went right out and sold $300,000 worth of roofs the first month. That would be at least $90,000 profit. Approximately half of that was mine, and of course, there was an office fee for Jerry, the company's owner, which was about $9,000. I was back in the saddle once again, making money hand over fist. It was crazy, the amount of money Jerry and I made together. We roofed half of the town, and I sold a quarter of the town a roof myself. I couldn't believe that it was so easy to make money. I was hooked again. Unfortunately, I was still addicted to everything. It got bad rather quickly because I started hanging out back in Ft. Worth, Texas, at the strip clubs. Unfortunately at the time, I was right back to the same old song and dance. One step forward and two steps back, fine cars, fine women, and fine dining. Amazingly within two months, I was back on top of the world. I didn't know at the time. But I was on the biggest bust ever!

I was a terrible addict, and my sin problem was becoming full-grown. When sin is full-grown, it brings forth death. I was addicted to power, position, and prestige; of course, these things are the world's measure of greatness. But most importantly, I was addicted to alcohol, women, and strip clubs. Further, I've got a bachelor's pad the size of Graceland, and now I have decided to complicate my life by getting married to my third wife, Nicki. Throwing caution to the wind, I went out and bought a brand new $70,000 truck. Sadly, I had strippers stashed in two different high-end apartments. It was horrible, and I married this sweet girl and immediately cheated on her. I wanted my cake and to eat it too. Then after being out of prison for sixteen months, I got mad at the owner of the company. There was a dispute over money. I then took a ride over to a job that I was doing at the time. I had the customer pay me in cash. I signed a receipt, doing that to protect the customer, and I kept $18,000 cash, meaning I stole the money by the law's definition. You can't do that, even though the company owed me at least $23,000. I used that reasoning to justify my actions. Very simply, I was completely wrong to do that. That is not right to do to anyone. So here I go again, right back to prison.

I had just gotten married on June 28, 2013, to my third wife, Nicki. This was in July 2013. I remember going out on a weekend binge shortly after I had that dispute with my business partner Jerry. I began partying all weekend with a couple of girls around Arlington and Ft. Worth, Texas. We all wound up at the top of the OmniAmerican Hotel. It was a very expensive hotel. I really liked to party hard back then, and I felt like a rock star most nights. I partied more money that weekend than most American families make in a month. It was approximately $5,000-$6,000! I remember waking up Sunday morning and looking at these two naked girls in bed with me. I began thinking, "Man Nicki is going to divorce me." The reason was that that night, in a drunken stupor, I threw my $3,500 wedding ring out the window of the Hummer stretch limo I was in, not to mention I was partying all weekend. I remember thinking wow, this is absurd. I quickly grabbed a fifth of Jim Beam and thought to myself. I got drunk to cope with the guilt, shame, and condemnation I felt. I then kicked the girls out of the room we were in. But not before snorting a line of cocaine off one of their chest. I walked downstairs and got in my $70,000 truck. I put on a Tracy Lawrence song and drove toward my house. I was in a really bad frame of mind.

## DIVINE REVELATION

Before I got there, I decided to stop at a church on the same exit. I often took that exit on the way home. As I got out of my truck, it was as hot as it could get in the great state of Texas that day. The heat just hit me right in the face as I opened the cab door. I don't know why I stopped. I wasn't a man of faith. But, as I talked to the pastor of the church about my situation, I explained to him how I had been living in thorough detail. I looked like a billion dollars on the outside, but on the inside, I was as dead as a man in the grave. I was as completely bankrupt as a human could get. I didn't even feel human anymore as I finished telling my story, sitting in that church high on cocaine and half drunk on Jim Beam whiskey. I was ashamed of myself. I couldn't even look at the pastor after telling him my story. Then the weirdest thing happened to me, when I looked up, I saw the look on the pastor's face. *He was shocked!* I mean, he was speechless. He looked me right in the eyes and said, "Son, you're poised for a miracle." I said, "This guy's a crackpot."

In retrospect, I didn't know what he meant. I had begged and pleaded with God my whole life to deliver me from my addictions and compulsions, and the preacher of this huge church simply says, "Your poised for a Miracle!" What I found out later was what that preacher told me was that I had placed myself beyond the point of human aid. *I needed a miracle to come back from where I was.* I needed the kind of help only God could provide! You see, that preacher knew what I didn't. He knew that only God could help me out of the fix I was in. I'm sure it is safe to say that the pastor also knew I would probably die a premature death if I didn't get help quickly. As I drove away from that church, I realized how hopeless I really was. It was the worst feeling I had ever felt to that point in my life. I had never known utter hopelessness and despair like I had come to know on that day.

As I got to my house, my wife was there. I did a combination of oxycodone and cocaine before I went inside. I also slammed down a couple of beers. Which, by the way, is a terrible combination of illicit drugs. You should never take uppers and downers together. They can stop your heart. I waited 10 minutes in my driveway. You couldn't see my truck in the driveway from inside the house. I walked in and said, "Hey baby, I'm home," as if I was about to get the husband of the decade award. Nicki rocked back from pit road to victory lane and slapped me right in the mouth. I regained my composure and innocently said, "What is that for?" She slapped me again! At that point, I needed the fifth of Jim Beam I forgot at the hotel room just to numb the pain. The good thing was I had taken two fifteen milligram Oxycodone painkillers before I went in. She told me she wanted a divorce. The sad part about all this is that we were not even married for two months. Wow! I could have messed up a cup of black coffee back then. I had it all figured out, though. You couldn't tell me anything. I HAD SET MYSELF UP AS THE GOD OF MY LIFE, MY WORLD, AND NOBODY WAS GOING TO DETHRONE ME.

## ANOTHER RISE TO THE TOP

One month later, the cops and detectives surrounded my house and took me to jail for Grand Theft, and sent me back to prison for four years. Amazingly, Nicki stayed married to me while I was in prison. All the while, I was incarcerated for forty months on that forty-eight-month sentence. I finally got out of prison on April 17, 2017. It was a Wednesday, and I was at a buddy of mine's office in Lewisville, Texas, on Friday. On Monday, I was back to making $10,000 a month. Unbelievable! After a couple of months of working for my buddy, the next thing I knew, I'm telling him after an argument, that I quit. I then started working for a company out of Houston, TX, as their new General Manager. At the time, I was working in the richest part of north Dallas in a billion-dollar hail storm. Some of the towns that I was working in were Plano, Frisco, Allen, Mckinney, Southlake, and Trophy Club. I quickly started making over $30,000 a month. Amazingly, I was doing better than ever, and still with my third wife, Nicki, who was still by my side waiting for me to change. The owner of the company was amazed at how much I was selling! He was making a small fortune off me, at least $60,000 a month.

I was running wide open like always! I was responsible for everything north of Houston, Texas, for my new boss Bobby. Now, I must remind you that I had only eight months of parole. But I had already violated that in thirty days by cutting my curfew monitor off my leg and drinking. It was Terrible! There I was, ripping, running, and gunning, and I'm no longer in the small houses of Mineral Wells, Texas. I'm in the huge homes of North Dallas now. The neighborhoods I worked in was where the professional sports players lived. Some of the players from the Dallas Cowboys, Dallas Stars, and Texas Rangers lived there. I was making more money in one sale than in five in other neighborhoods. The greatest thing of all was that the people loved me there. It was a salesman's dream! The first three hours I worked for this company that I'm talking about, I sold a job that made a $16,000 profit. It was absolutely insane, the amount of money I was making and how easy it was. I made about eight thousand dollars on that first sale.

## THE DEAL OF A LIFETIME

It was around this time that I started working day and night. I was living the dream. Surprisingly, I was somehow drinking a lot less. But unfortunately, I had become a ghost husband again. In other words, I was a slave to my job, money, success, and a slew of addictions and compulsions. One thing that I know for certain, old habits die hard. Nevertheless, I kept on making a fortune, and by chance, I met a real estate investor. We struck up a deal on over one hundred houses. My boss gave me a check for $50,000 that very day. That was the front half of my commission on that deal. It was very common for me to hide money from my wife. I did this because, in my world, I never trusted anyone. As I look back on my former life, I realize why! I judged the world by my actions. I was dishonest, so the rest of the world had to be dishonest and unworthy of my trust. I was completely wrong! But, be that as it may. I was living a dream, and yes, it was a bad one! The only problem was that I wasn't sure if it was a good or a bad dream back then. Most of the time back then, my dreams were nightmares. I was wanted on a parole violation. Therefore, I didn't want the company to owe me a lot of money on the back end of my commission. I was thinking about everything one day and decided to slow down a little bit.

My main problem, which was a good problem to have, was that I had made so many contacts with the jobs that I sold, that the jobs and money just kept rolling in, one right after another. On August 27, 2017, after making right under $5,000 that day, I decided to go back home. I called my wife and told my her, "I'm coming home." She said, "Thank God." Nicki told me to meet her at her daughter's house. I was driving to meet her at my stepdaughter's house in Arlington, Texas. I had to stop by my house on the way and get cleaned up for the party. It was about a sixty-minute drive from where I was in Mckinney, TX. I hadn't touched a drop of alcohol in three months. The disease of addiction was strong on that day. I knew I couldn't drink at the party because my wife wouldn't let me. I quickly concocted a plan to get drunk before I got to the party because she would be drinking and couldn't smell the alcohol on me. Right there on that drive home, I implemented that plan to get drunk in ninety minutes. On the drive home, I drank five to six beers. I stopped at my house and quickly drank two more quarts. I drove twenty minutes to my stepdaughter Angela's house in Arlington, Texas, having had two more quarts of beer before I got there. I got to the party, and all was utopia. I was heavily intoxicated!

It really relieved a lot of pressure on me to be at that party drunk. There were about fifty people at my stepdaughter's house when I arrived. I was the life of the party. I had on designer clothing from head to toe. Versace was always my favorite, and I was even wearing a $500 pair of Versace sunglasses on this particular night. I'm almost certain, looking back now, that I looked stupid wearing my sunglasses at nighttime. A big fight broke out between my thirty-one-year-old stepdaughter and her nineteen-year-old boyfriend. I got in my brand spanking new Ford Escape that I had just bought. My wife needed something to haul three grandchildren around in. I ended up leaving the party because I was scared the cops would come. I wound up going to my old stomping ground in the Ft. Worth Stockyards. In my mind, I was thinking my wife was going to stay with our daughter that night. But, just in case she didn't, I figured that I would stay longer than two hours at this strip club that I was at. I spent about $1200 in a matter of about two hours there. But I was trying to please my wife by driving all the way back to my house that evening. Generally speaking, I'm was not drinking and driving anymore. I quit doing that after my second arrest for driving under the influence. It was common after my second arrest for D.U.I. to get a hotel near the bar I was drinking at or call a limousine service to chauffeur me around town.

# A HIGH-SPEED CHASE

On this particular night though, I decided to drive twenty miles to get home. The whole time I was at the club, Nicki was calling me nonstop. I finally made it home safely and breathed a sigh of relief. I would have never dreamed what would happen to me on this evening. As I drove into the parking lot, I saw Nicki's car. She was waiting on me. I walked up the stairs to our apartment and slid the key into the door. The door was locked, had a chain on it, and to make matters worse, she would not let me in. But I didn't want to cause a scene because I was wanted by parole. I closed the door and walked through the parking lot to my vehicle. I got in my car and stopped at the stop sign perfectly. It was a beautiful summer night. I drove about half a mile and stopped at a red light. I looked up, waiting for the light to turn green, and saw a Bedford police officer stop in the middle of the road. The cop looked right at me and did a U-turn in the middle of the road. Then the cop attempted to pull me over.

The cops told me that they were arresting me for a high-speed chase and driving while intoxicated. After they arrested me, they transferred me to the Tarrant County Jail. But I was not able to bond out because I had a parole hold. My discharge date for parole was in December and it was only August 27th. The sad part about this whole thing is that it was only one day before my youngest daughter's birthday. What a dad! I was reckless, careless, and irresponsible. I was owed over $60,000 in commission, and the roof jobs were steadily rolling in. The owner of the company tried to buy me out of trouble, but all the money in the world couldn't free me from my troubles. I soon realized that I had to sit in jail until December 22, 2017. I then hired the best parole attorney in the state. He filed some motions with the courts and forced them to discharge me from parole. Then on December 31, 2017, after sitting in the Tarrant County Jail for four months, I posted bond on my charges.

At approximately 11:30 that night, the guard handed me $2,200 in cash, and we walked downstairs and out the door. My wife Nicki was waiting there to pick me up. Unbeknownst to me at the time. I was getting in the car with not only the woman I was trying to love. I say it like that because I wasn't constitutionally capable of loving myself or anyone else for that matter. She also called the cops the night I got arrested and lied about me, and then kept it a secret until I found out about it on my own. She had called the cops once before I ever got there. Then a second time, after I got home that night from the strip club, she called the cops again. I didn't figure this out until about a month after I got out of jail, went to my attorney's office, and saw the motion to discover the evidence against me. We were preparing for trial, and the prosecutor didn't like me. I want to make sure you understand something, though. Although Nicki lied to the cops, my ex-wife would have never done that if I would have come home that night like I was supposed to. I take full responsibility for my actions. I eventually went to my first court appearance from the free world, and they offered me fifteen years. This was the sixth time they had made that offer on these charges.

Allow me to paint a very clear picture for you. I just did over eight and a half years on eleven years worth of sentences. I should have only done about three years. They were nonviolent charges. Let me get this straight. The prosecutor now wants me to do a fifteen-year prison sentence. That means I would have to do twelve more years on that sentence by the standard they set on my previous convictions. Let me get this right, you mean to tell me that I have to do almost twenty-one years on nonviolent sentences? I know people who have killed people in accidents caused because they were driving drunk. Texas law carries a maximum penalty of ten years for involuntary manslaughter, which is the charge they give you for killing someone while drinking and driving. Make no mistake, I get it. I'm not downplaying my actions. I assure you that I accept full responsibility for my actions. I'm just saying that I don't feel like that amount of time is justifiable for nonviolent crimes. The absolute truth about all this is that, it is none of my business what they do to other people. My actions are my business. I'm trying to get you to understand the difference between my thought process then and now.

## PARTYING IN HOLLYWOOD

My attorney called me to his office one day and told me the district attorney would not come off the fifteen-year plea bargain agreement. I decided to jump bail and make a run for it. I decided to go home one day and get all of my stuff. I decided to drain five bank accounts of all the money in them at the time. The reason being was that I was about to board an American Airlines jet for Hollywood, California. I drove my wife Nicki's car to the airport; I got about a mile from the airport and poured five pounds of sugar into the gas tank. I got out of her car that I valet parked on purpose, out of spite, I knew she wouldn't be able to find the car, and by the time she does figure out where it is, she will need a loan to get her car back that I paid for. I look at the valet guy and say, "Leave it running." The valet guy just kind of looked at me, shocked. I boarded the plane for Hollywood, California. The plane landed five hours later at LAX airport in Los Angeles, California. I caught a cab and set up shop at a beautiful condo behind the Chinese Theater. It was right on the corner of Hollywood Boulevard and Orange Street. California was great and everything was very expensive out there. I started partying hard with alcohol, cocaine, and women. The California women loved me and they were all over me white on rice.

The very first night off the plane. I was standing at a bar watching the Super Bowl. I heard a girl behind me ask a friend for a napkin. Then her friend said, "there isn't any." So being the true southern gentleman I am, I reached over to grab a handful of napkins from the bar, just to be kind. I was dressed to kill, as always. I'm drunk and I was very cocky that day. As I looked back to give the napkins to the girl's friend, I said, "Here you go, ladies. Does someone need a napkin?" Then this beautiful young brunette that needed the napkin heard me speak with that slow southern drawl. She came around the table and got right in my face. She was about two inches from me, and I could smell the Margarita she was drinking on her breath. She said, "Where are you from?" I said, "Texas." Before I barely got the words out of my mouth, she lip-locked me. I partied all night with her and three other girls. In retrospect, I must say, "I was out of control." It was crazy, and I definitely was crazier than ever. I lived in the bars for thirty days. I was begging for mercy by the time I came to my senses.

I started partying at all the strip clubs in Los Angeles, California. I was mainly just drinking copious amounts of alcohol. The only problem was that I was always around women, which was a constant trigger for me to drink and do drugs. That made me want to do cocaine to stay up and party with them. After about two weeks of partying at 2-3 strip clubs a day. I took a break and suddenly came to this startling realization: all that I had done was prolong the inevitable. I had just ruined a third marriage and lost a wonderful wife that really loved me.

I also was trying to come to terms with going back to prison. At the time, they were still offering me fifteen years as a plea agreement. I had jumped bail, and bounty hunters were looking for me. My youngest daughter was only eleven years old at the time and she loved and adored me more than anything. Sadly she doesn't even know me. I was thinking about this the whole time I was on the run and came to this realization. That she will never know me if they give me fifteen years in prison. I had to drink just to live with myself and the fact that I was a complete washout at forty years old.

## CHOOSING TO BECOME A HEROIN ADDICT

I was addicted to the party life. I then came to know darkness like I had never known before. I realized I needed to pull it together. I also realized that mentally, physically, and emotionally, I was a recipe for disaster. I called my brother, and at the time, he owed me $4,000. My brother had stolen this money from me while I was in jail on my third Driving While Intoxicated charge. I decided to fly back to Texas. I drove over to my brother's house. I walked in the door and asked him about the money he had stolen from me months earlier. Then he dropped a bombshell on me. He told me that "He was dying of liver cancer and he was also addicted to heroin." My brother explained that he had spent my four thousand dollars on drugs. I looked over in the closet, and my brother's girlfriend was making him up a shot of heroin. She draws up a shot in front of me, and my brother injects himself with it. He uses the pain from liver cancer to justify his heroin addiction. I'm completely devastated and it was terrible to watch my brother go through heroin addiction. On top of all that was going on in my life. My closest brother looks me right in the eyes and tells me he's going to die soon and is a heroin addict. In comparison to what he used to be, he is only the shell of the person he once was. His gaze was fixed on me as he got his fix. When he asked "If I wanted some," I quickly replied, "No," with a four-letter expletive attached. I got in my truck, and I was in tears. I returned to my old stomping grounds and got knocked down, slobbering drunk.

I went back the next day to check on my brother. I got there and walked in; it was a perfect replay of the scene from the previous night. The only problem I had this time was that I was drunk. He had his girl making him up a shot of heroin again. He asked me again, "If I wanted some." I said, "Yes!" He immediately drew up four units in a syringe and injected the heroin into my right arm. Thirty seconds later, I feel the euphoria from the opiates. I went back to my place that night.

I woke up the next morning and returned to my brother's house. He injected me with seven units this time. Eight hours later, he injected me again with seven more. Then after a week, I moved to 12 units, three times a day. After about two months. I was injecting heroin six times a day, 20 units each time. It got so bad that I would wake up in the middle of the night every three hours injecting heroin. I suddenly realized one day that I was doomed! I'm hooked and now I'm a drug addict!

## SETTING MYSELF UP FOR FAILURE WITH MONEY

I concocted a plan to open up two roofing offices. One in Bedford, Texas, and I opened one up in Wichita Falls, Texas. I need a lot of money because I have at least a $3,000-a-month heroin habit, and I know heroin is a loaded word. There are very few people who come back from that kind of lifestyle. It was the worst mistake I ever made, or was it? You see my good friend. I could always rationalize and justify my drinking. It was legal and I only drank a few days a week. Although in those couple days a week, I drank enough alcohol for a month. At least eight times a month. But now the poor boy from Arlington, Texas, has bit off more than he can chew with heroin.

I started making about $7,000 a week. But the only problem was that I had mismanaged all my money. I had plenty of money, but I spent it on women, alcohol, and heroin! It was terrible, and I did the best I could for myself at the time. I shacked up with a girl named Toya in Wichita Falls, and I hid my heroin habit from her through my diabetes. Toya was a sweet girl. But I was just very sick and self-destructive and I knew it. I broke up with her a couple of months later. I had to regularly check my blood sugar and take insulin so it didn't throw up a red flag that I had needles. I went on a gambling spree for three months in two different states. I won quite a bit of money. I then decided to go to Shreveport, Louisiana. I set up shop at the Horseshoe Casino. It was a very nice place! You do get what you pay for there. I got so lonely that I went to a very popular dating site online. I met a girl named Angie there. We talked on the phone, and then she came to the casino to meet me one day.

She called me from the parking lot when she got there. I remember it like it was yesterday. I was dressed from head to toe in Versace and as I stepped off the elevator, I could see my reflection on the Italian Marble floor. I looked up and saw the valet guy that always took care of me there. He then looked right at me and said, "You need your car, Mr. Odell?" I said, "No." As I round the corner, I can smell the great food from the steak house. I got a pocketful of bank envelopes. They have crisp, clean, one hundred dollar bills in them, about $30,000 worth. I got $2,000 in twenty dollar bills in my left pocket. As I rounded the corner, I looked up, and bingo! There she was, sitting on a bench, waiting for me. She looked up and saw me, she smiled real big and I saw a gleam in her eyes. She jumped up and ran to me and we hugged one another. I say to myself as she hugs me, "Don't rub me while you're hugging me." It was to late. She already has and now my shirt was wrinkled. Insanity! We had a great time that night.

The first night my new girlfriend Angie and I were together, I set a bad precedent. We gambled thousands of dollars on the slots and I always hated slots. Playing the slots is like playing the Powerball lottery. It is all luck! We ended up staying together and amazingly we didn't sleep together. She is a good woman and way to good for a guy like me. After about a week, we decided to shack up together on the ritzy side of Shreveport, Louisiana. I was making a lot of money back then. But I was spending a lot also. I'm living like I'm in the Billionaires Boys Club. But the only problem was that I was not even making millions. I bought her some diamonds, which were of all colors, shapes, and sizes. She was impressed, but we were partying every night in Mercedes party buses, Cadillac D.T.S. limos, and Lincoln Continental stretch limos. I was completely out of control. At this particular point in my life, I was paying double for the price of my heroin. I started carrying two pistols around and the Bounty Hunters were kicking doors down in Texas looking for me. I was on a terrible binge and was using copious amounts of heroin and alcohol to numb me to the truth. The truth was I didn't feel loved, needed, or wanted. But I felt completely doomed! I felt hopeless and my only hope was in alcohol, heroin, women, and money. Sadly, these things only gave me false hope, a pure and perfect conditional hope, which is no hope at all. There is only one true hope, and that is Jesus Christ.

## BEGINNING OF THE END

After a few months, I heard of a category-5 hurricane that slammed into the Florida panhandle. I was not licensed to work in the state of Florida. But I had general liability insurance through my company, which is a requirement to get licensed through the state of Florida to become a contractor. I came up with this grand plan to go to work with someone else. I googled roofing contractors on my phone, and a phone number to one in Panama City Beach, Florida, popped up. I called it and a guy answered the phone. I then asked him, "Are you hiring sales representatives?" He said, "I'm an insurance adjuster. I bought this phone a few nights ago because all the Verizon towers blew down in the storm. I have had people calling me left and right to get their roofs tarped." He then asked, "Do you want the numbers of all the people who called me?" I said, "Sure and I will pay you 10% of the total contract price for all the jobs you send me." He ended up giving me approximately 10-12 jobs in one week. He then started having people call me before I ever got there. Shortly after, I struck up the deal of a lifetime with my new adjuster friend. I told him that I would be there in five days. He explained that I could stay in this condo he rented. We agreed on the price of one thousand dollars a month. I told my girlfriend Angie that I was going to Florida and she was crushed but soon realized it was necessary.

As I'm driving down the highway towards the Gulf Coast I realize that I'm a heroin addict, alcoholic, liar, cheat, thief, con, swindler, and master manipulator. I lived in total darkness, and I was hopeless. There was nothing left of me but the shell of what used to be that bright young kid from Arlington, Texas. One might say, "Life as I knew it was coming to an end." One thing about it was that I knew I was beat with the heroin addiction. But I would fight and press on to the bitter end. I would do the most foolish thing a human can do: try to fight sin on their own accord. A man has to be very proud and greatly deceived by Satan to think he can solve his own sin problem. My death was near and I welcomed it with all of my heart. I didn't know any other life and I was tired and retired. I had fought so hard and for so long, and was struggling from every angle in life, that it never occurred to me that I needed to surrender my heart and life to Christ to solve my sin problem and that would have solved all of my problems. The world had taught me how to fight to the bitter end. But nobody ever taught me how to surrender. In other words, give up. The sad truth is that I really didn't know how to surrender.

# CHAPTER 5

---◆◆◇◆◆---

# ADDICTION

As I woke up that morning and I was getting ready to depart for Florida. I knew my girlfriend was going to be devastated. I was leaving to chase a hurricane that slammed into the Florida panhandle. She had seen the fruits of my labor. But she had never seen how much money I made in a hurricane. She believed in me and trusted me because I put up a good front with her. But my whole life and our relationship were based on lies on my part. She also didn't know I was a heroin addict. I toned my drinking way down when we first met. There was no need for me to consume alcohol anymore. The reason why is that I was doing entirely too much heroin. But the only problem was we were in a different limo three or four nights a week, so I kept on drinking, but not as much. I created a false reality for us. *The truth is I was always down in my mind. I would create this false reality so I could live with the facts that I was an alcoholic, drug addict, liar, cheat, thief, con, swindler, and master manipulator. Simply put. I was never ok with myself. As far back as I can remember, I have always wanted to be someone else. I used people, places, and things to feel the way I wanted. Even if it was moment by moment. I was addicted to everything I ever put my hands on. I was addicted to sugar, caffeine, alcohol, drugs, money, power, success, position, prestige, and pornography. It was terrible.* I didn't know who I was anymore. I heard another addict named Chris' mentor, who works for a Rhode Island newspaper, say it best. He said, *"You go into a movie. It is supposed to be a feel-good movie. But, toward the end of the movie, something goes terribly wrong, and you walk out with this sick feeling in your stomach."* That is a great analogy for my former life! That is exactly what happened to me. I had it all and ruined it because of my selfishness and ignorance of the word of God. A fool and his money soon part. I was definitely a fool.

I had overcome the ghetto, being poor, and made it to the top of the residential roofing industry. There I was, making all this money at nineteen years old. I was chasing hail storms and hurricanes all over the country for roughly eleven years. Then the bottom falls out, and everyone walks away from me. All of my wives, kids, and family, and rightfully so. But now I'm a heroin addict and I'm a fugitive from justice. There wasn't any way on God's green earth that I was going to come back from that kind of story on my own accord. The reason why is really very simple. If I had been that smart, I would not have been in that predicament in the first place. Wow! How sad.

So what was my problem? I had a spiritual problem. Dr. William Silkworth called it a spiritual malady. Malady means bad heart, ill, and diseased. More to the point, I had a sin problem. Unless I could understand that addiction is a disease, it is not a moral issue or a lack of willpower, I would succumb to the disease of addiction and die.

## A DIVINE APPOINTMENT

As soon as I woke up, I put on those designer jeans, my favorite black golf shirt, and those brand new red, white, and black Puma shoes I liked. The things that were about to happen to me were beyond my imagination. After all those years I had begged and pleaded with God to deliver me from selfishness and self-centeredness, I begged him to help me change. I was closer to my miracle than I ever realized. The only problem was that I wasn't willing to change. In the end, I finally figured out that all I was doing was giving God lip service. "The heart *is* deceitful above all *things,* And desperately wicked; Who can know it" (Jeremiah 17:9, NKJV)? I needed a heart transplant by the greatest heart surgeon in all creation. Looking back now, my Lord and my God was the only one that could help me. You couldn't fly a helicopter into the fortress that I had built around my heart.

Somewhere deep down inside of me was that scared little boy that wouldn't come out, whose earthly father had rejected him and wouldn't validate he loved his son. I was stuck and crying out for help all those years. I found the bottle, or maybe it found me and that didn't work. I did heroin six times a day; sorry, that wouldn't stop the pain either. I needed help to get out of the fortress that I had built around my heart. All the alcohol, drugs, and money on Earth couldn't have saved me. I was sinking fast and running out of time. I also tried women, which went south quick, fast, and in a hurry. I knew when I woke up that day that I had a seven-hour drive before I would pull over somewhere in Mississippi. I didn't know it at the time. But I had a divine appointment with the living God and Creator of all things. He was positioning me perfectly for a miracle that the whole world would know about. I also didn't know at the time. But the good Lord had already assembled a rescue team that started with his son Jesus Christ dying on the cross for my sins over two thousand years ago.

God knew I wasn't strong enough in my faith. So the good Lord would use humans carefully placed in all the right places to help me. Little did I know at the time, these were special humans. They were genuine Christians, with a genuine love for all of humanity, just like Jesus Christ. This is because God is in them, acting according to his will and good pleasure. These people God put in my path were absolutely surrendered, 100% totally committed followers of Jesus Christ. I really stress the followers' part because of the measure of their surrender. The Most High God could reach out to the most broken human beings on earth and love them back from the gates of a self-induced torturous hell they were living in. God's resurrection power could flow freely to and through these people to help them and I receive his love, grace, and mercy.

I can see the angels of Heaven applauding and singing glory be to God in its highest because I would truly repent! It was all because a sinner would soon turn from the error of his ways. I remember it was a gloomy day in October. I was driving down highway forty-nine, coming out of Shreveport, Louisiana. I stopped at a gas station and did some heroin. As I walked out of the gas station, something said, "Go back home." I thought to myself, I will make at least ten to fifteen thousand dollars in the next week. I'm going to Panama City Beach, Florida! I remember listening to a guy on my radio named Tracy Lawrence. Tracy and I go back all the way to 1991. It was a song called "If the good die young."

My life kind of flashed before my eyes. I remember thinking there has got to be more to life than this. I thought about my ex-wife Nicki, who I was still married to at the time. I remember thinking, there goes another good wife. I can remember shaking my head in disgust. I was still married to my third wife but separated from her and engaged to a girl back in Wichita Falls,

Texas. All the while, I'm engaged to this girl in Shreveport, Louisiana! Wow, how was I going to pull that off? My whole life was one big lie! I didn't know what to do to fix it either. Which is precisely my point, an addict living in active addiction cannot maintain integrity. As addicts, we also all lead double lives, become pathological liars, and master manipulators. That was what I had become, which is a very graceful way of putting it. This is the Biology of Addiction below.

## THE DISEASE OF ADDICTION

Biology of Addiction

Biology (genes and epigenetics)

+

Stress (especially trauma)

+

DRUG

= Risk of Addiction

*"One in ten people will have a serious substance use problem in his or her lifetime. Thirty-three percent of us will be directly affected by addiction. Around fifty percent of emergency room admissions are related to substance abuse. The cost of drug abuse and addiction to society, combining healthcare costs, productivity loss, crime, incarceration, and drug-related law enforcement, is close to 740 billion dollars a year. What is addiction? The official American Society of Addiction Medicine (ASAM) definition is "a treatable, chronic medical disease involving complex interactions among brain circuits, genetics,*

*the environment, and an individual's life experiences. People with addiction use substances or engage in behaviors that become compulsive and often continue despite harmful consequences" (American Society of Addiction Medicine, 2019). Active addiction is an imbalance in brain chemistry, starting with a genetic predisposition made susceptible to stress, inflammation, chronic use, and inability to achieve stable brain chemistry because of chemical depletion. Self-medication to fill a void or treat a physical or mental symptom may result in addiction. This is considered self-medicating gone wrong. Addiction is not bad people doing bad things. Addiction is not a choice. Addiction is similar to other chronic illnesses, such as heart disease or diabetes, which disrupt the underlying organ's normal, healthy functioning, causing very harmful consequences. These diseases are preventable and treatable, but if left untreated, they can relapse and impact people for a lifetime (Smith, 2012). Simply put, addiction is a chronic, relapsing illness causing impaired control, continued use despite harm, compulsive use, and cravings (Fraser et al.,2014). Chronic means that it is a long-lasting condition that can be controlled but not cured. The relapse rate in drug addiction is 40 to 60%. Hypertension has a 50 to 70% relapse rate. Type 1 Diabetes has a 30 to 50% relapse rate. Many diseases have regular relapses or recurrences of the condition after a period of remission. It is interesting to compare addiction to other chronic relapsing diseases, such as cancer or heart disease. When cancer relapses, we usually blame the medication or disease, and then we do an aggressive workup to find better, more effective treatments to protect the patient from the disease. But, in addiction relapse, we historically blame the patient" (National Institute on Drug Abuse 2018)!* Remember I said that if you use or abuse substances before you are eighteen years old, you are sixty-five percent more likely to become an addict as an adult. I have used and abused drugs and alcohol since I was twelve years old. This is why addiction is a disease. When a doctor diagnoses you with a disease, he or she uses what they call a Disease Causal Model. It goes like this for the disease of addiction.

## Disease Causal Model

Organ: (Brain)

+

Defect: The breakdown in communication between the

NAc and left orbitofrontal cortex

+

Symptoms: Chemical use despite consequences

This is how a doctor diagnoses a disease. You have an organ, which in addiction is the brain. You have a deformity in the organ, which is the breakdown in communication between the nucleus accumbens *septi* and the left orbitofrontal cortex in the brain. Then you have symptoms which are chemical use despite consequences, loss of control, tolerance and withdrawal, and cravings (Caravella). In layman's terms, this is low blood flow to the frontal cortex or hypofrontality. This is exactly what happens in the brain when you use addictive substances. When you use illicit drugs your brain secretes a neurotransmitter called Dopamine. *"This neurotransmitter gives you a sense of well-being. Dopamine is the key player, as all addictive drugs release dopamine in the reward circuit. Dopamine is the alarm, causing wakefulness, focus, reward, and pleasure. To understand addiction, we must have a basic understanding of brain reward circuits. There are natural rewards, like natural pleasures in life, in which all five senses provide input. Finding rewards in life establishes habits that dominate our behaviors. Reward is signaled by dopamine release. Chocolate, exercise, orgasm, being kind, and even drugs elevate dopamine release. The problem comes in when the dopamine spike is too high, and resilience is too low, causing poor dopamine tone. The addicted brain has a problem with resetting to baseline. The nonaddicted brain, when getting a dopamine reward with a drug, chocolate, orgasm, and the like, experiences a spike, and then the dopamine comes back down to its normal point. The addicted brain gets a more intense spike, and dopamine levels plummet below normal levels. Another dopamine spike may afford feelings of a normal level, but dopamine levels are ratcheted down with every spike and fall. Eventually, the cycle leaves the baseline of an addict's brain dopamine at virtually zero. The only way the addict can get close to feeling normal again is to keep using the drug. This is what an addict struggles with daily, to feel like they are surviving. It becomes a survival drive to use, like hunger, thirst, sleep, or even breathing" (Hooked, 2016). Another way to simply put it, is the addict is being chemically controlled. Meaning the addict has crossed the fine line from being a drug user or abuser to being an addict. This is why. When an addict uses and or abuses drugs long enough. Every time an addict uses drugs, their brain's dopamine levels soar from the use of illicit drugs. The addict gets anywhere from 100 to 1000 times more of a dopamine response from the use of illicit drugs then they normally would from chocolate, orgasm, exercise, or being kind. The brain, in effect, says, "I have released too much dopamine." Then it releases less and less. Ratcheting your dopamine tone to zero. Now in the deep center of the brain lies the midbrain, where the pleasure centers and reward pathways exist. The pleasure reward center consists of the ventral tegmentum and the nucleus accumbens, which are directly linked to the frontal lobe (specifically the prefrontal cortex and frontal cortex), where decision making, social behavior, planning, and general executive functioning are carried out. Once you lack a dopaminergic response. In other words, the dopamine tone ratchets down to zero. The addict has to have their drug of most effective reward to feel anywhere near normal. They also have lost top-down control" (Hooked, 2016).* In other words, the intellectual part of the brain has been hijacked by the midbrain, which is the fight-or-flight part of the brain. It is what tells you, in effect, I need food, clothing, water, shelter, and sex. Except now, drugs just went to the top of that list. In layman's terms, your body is associating that drug with survival, and there's a role reversal between the prefrontal cortex/frontal cortex and the midbrain. When this occurs, the midbrain is four to five times stronger than the frontal cortex, driving you to use your drug of choice to get a dopamine response. This is why a mother, with maternal instinct, who would normally give her life for her children. When she gets addicted to chemicals, she will neglect her children and buy drugs before she buys food for her children.

This is also why I have decided to devote my whole life to helping addicts. I will become a Licensed Alcohol and Drug Counselor by the year 2028. It is my main goal every day to go into life with the right perception, and that is so that I can add value to the lives of those around me, namely addicts. You have got to understand something. I really wanted to be a good person even in my darkest hour. I was just very selfish, self-centered, and addicted.

As a recovered addict myself, I realize that I was a very unlovely person. But on the flip side of things, I understand why now. Therefore when I see other addicts in active addiction, who are very unlovely creatures, I understand how to help them. I understand that in active addiction, we all lead a double life, become pathological liars, and master manipulators. I realize addicts cannot maintain integrity; their whole life revolves around what they can get from the people, places, and things around them. Their whole life is about getting their drug of most effective reward because it is no longer a choice. Addicts demand everything and give very little, only enough to get what they want!

That was exactly what my problem was in my former life. The great thing about possessing this experience is that it gives me the ability to give any addict I meet an abundance of patience, love, grace, and mercy. The reason why is that I understand the disease of addiction completely from every angle. I also understand the spiritual malady of addiction; at its root, addiction is a sin problem. When this sin problem, that we call addiction is full-grown, it then gives birth to death. God makes that possible!

"The wages of sin is death, but the free gift of God is eternal life in Christ Jesus our Lord" (Romans 6:23). The addict is the god of his life and everyone and everything around him or her. They are greatly deceived, and the sad state of their world is that they are too chemically controlled to see that their drug use affects the only two things that truly matter in life. That is their relationship with God and their relationships with their fellow man. There is one thing that makes life worth living, relationships! That was one of the main problems in my former life. I really believed I didn't need anyone or anything, and that was what I told myself every day. I needed money, and that was it. My life had been deceived by Satan, the god of this world, who had led me to believe I was meant to live my life alone, isolated, and chemically controlled. Because I chose ignorance over knowledge, I was always searching for dopaminergic responses in sex, alcohol, and drugs. It was all due to my ignorance, a lack of knowledge about the truth. The Bible is the truth.

The solution to all of my problems and the whole world's problems were all right there the whole time in God's word. The only question was would I receive Jesus Christ, the living word, which is the way, the truth, and the life (John 14:6). I wanted to be free from my slavery to sin. But I didn't realize that this only comes through these three truths; Jesus Christ, the gospel truth, and God's Holy Spirit of truth. The Bible says those the son sets free are indeed free. But would I receive the truth before it was too late?

As I drove down the highway in Louisiana that fateful day, it started getting dark. I remember passing a casino. Something deep inside me said, "Stop there for the night." I quickly shrugged it off. Something said, "Stop here." Then the weirdest thing happened. A feeling of dread came over me. Almost as if there was a presence of evil with me. That same presence I could feel in that dream I told you about that I had on August 17, 1991. It was with me in the truck. I have never told anyone about this. I wanted to get out of the truck, but I kept driving. I stopped to get something to drink. I remember thinking I'm going back home. But the only problem was there was a lot of money to be made in Panama City Beach, Florida. Something just didn't seem right about the excursion I was taking that day though. I kept driving east toward the Gulf Coast. It was pitch black outside. I put in a Mark Chesnutt song and kept on driving. The phone rang while I was drifting off to a better place and a better time. I was on the coast of somewhere beautiful with my wife Nicki. We were on an island near Galveston, Texas, called Kema, right on the beach. My girlfriend quickly came over the phone. She was crying. She said, "Come home, baby." I wanted to say, "Yes," but I realized I couldn't. I realized that I not only needed the money, but I knew that I had this deal and that if it went right, it could be worth at least half a million dollars in the next six months. So I calmed her down by telling her that I would send her a plane ticket as soon as they got all the power and water turned on in Panama City Beach, Florida. I could have taken her with me right then. But I wanted to make sure my adjuster friend was the real deal. Shortly after our previous conversations that we already had. I determined there was a 99% chance that he was the real deal. I realized he was probably who he said he was, just by him talking as he did about the roofing business (not including having clients call me who he'd given my name to).

So, I looked up and saw a sign that said, "New Orleans twelve miles." I realized I was getting close to my destination and a gold mine. I also know that the moment I'm in Mississippi, I'm within striking distance of Panama City Beach, Florida. It had been a while since I had a shot of heroin. But I chose to keep driving and I was outside of Slidell, Louisiana, when I decided to do a shot of heroin going down the road. The shot of heroin was already made up in a syringe, and my veins are very good shooter veins. In other words, they are very easy to inject. I was driving with my knee, I inserted the needle in my vein and I made sure that I drew back blood in the syringe. I then plunged the heroin into my vein. I looked up and almost fell over dead! There was a cop behind me. I panicked but managed to remain calm. The cop speeds up past me and takes the exit. He looks right at me in the light. Almost as if he was trying to identify me.

I breathed a sigh of relief. I then say, "Thank God I'm not going to jail tonight." I think to myself, that just blew my high! I crossed over the bridge and saw a sign. It said welcome to the great state of Mississippi. I decided to pull over for the night. I needed another shot of dope and some sleep. I took the second exit off of the I-10 and was on highway 90. I saw a motel by a gas station and I pulled in. I said to myself, "I can finally get some rest."

# CHAPTER 6

---◆◆◇◆◆---

# THE CROSS AND DIVINE REVELATION

As I walked into the lobby of the motel. I looked up and saw an older lady. She smiled and said, "How may I help you, sir?" I asked her, "If she had any rooms available?" She said, "We have one available for seventy-five dollars plus tax." When she said that, I reached deep in my pocket and pulled out a bunch of one hundred dollar bills. I peeled one off and gave it to her. Then the weirdest thing happened to me. Something deep down inside me said, "Leave the money and go, do not stay here." It was so real that it was almost as if something had just whispered that in my ear. I ignored the voice because I needed another shot of heroin. I signed the receipt and checked into room number six shortly afterward. Coincidentally, the number six has a negative connotation in the Bible. Sometimes the number six is used to refer to a value falling short of a seven. For example, the number of the beast is 666, which represents its evil and having fallen short of the divinely perfect number seven. How fitting for a guy like I was in my former life. As I looked around the room, it was very disappointing. It was a dump. It was definitely not my style. But I decided it would have to do because it was almost midnight, and I was dog-tired. I stepped into the bathroom to get some water, but my blood sugar was low, because I'm a diabetic and take insulin. I then called my girlfriend back in Louisiana and told her where I was, my blood sugar was low, and that I will call her back in a few minutes. I hung up the phone. Then I went to the bathroom to get some water to mix up a shot of heroin. I opened the shoe box on my bed. I pulled out the nickel-plated .25 caliber pistol and the black 380 Ruger pistol. Then I started to get the heroin out of where it was hidden in a pair of socks. But suddenly, I am startled by a knock at the door, even though I haven't been in the room for ten minutes.

I immediately put the pistols back in the shoe box and quickly closed it. I usually would have looked out the window. But because I was in another state and had just checked into the room, I was sure that it was the manager of the motel. I opened the door, and I almost passed out! I was stunned, and much to my surprise, it was two Hancock County Sheriff Deputies. I almost slammed the door shut as I thought, I gotta get to that heroin. The cop points at my truck. He then asked me, "Is this your black dodge pickup?" I said, "Yes." He asked me, "If my name was James O'Dell." I said, "Yes." He quickly stepped up with the other officer and handcuffed me. The officer said, "You are not being arrested. You are being detained. We're confirming warrants right now, sir." As soon as the officer said that, I heard a woman's voice come over the officer's radio saying, "That suspect is wanted by multiple agencies in the state of Texas." I remember the officer looking at me sharply.

They did a security sweep of the room. I watched them open the shoe box on the bed and they immediately stepped out of the room and closed the door. They made a call on their cell phone anf that went to narcotic agents. Shortly after, they walked over to me and asked me, "Do we have permission to search your truck?" I refused permission and thought I would never cooperate with the police! But right then, my blood sugar was so low that I was about to pass out. I started kicking the door of the cop car. They opened the door, and I said, "I'm diabetic and my blood sugar is very low. Can you please bring me the crackers on the table?" They were kind of mad at me because I had just told them a few minutes earlier where to go and it wasn't to Heaven. At that time, we were waiting for the narcotic agents to get there. They would not uncuff me to eat. So, they began to feed me crackers on the side of the cop car in Bay St. Louis, Mississippi. It is now dawning on me that my life is over as I knew it. I'm doomed!

A couple of hours later, after waking up a judge in the middle of the night to get a search warrant. The narcotic agents showed up and searched everything. They found four grams of black tar heroin and two pistols. One of the pistols had hollow point bullets in it. I was then transported to the Hancock County Jail. They charged me with two counts of unlawful carrying of a firearm by a convicted felon, possession of heroin, and a dangerous weapon charge. It was crazy because they charged me with four felonies! I need you to understand something. This would be my twenty-fourth arrest. I was already convicted of seven felonies back in Texas. I already had the eighth and ninth felonies, which I had jumped bond on back in Texas. I was also convicted of a felony in the state of Ohio and now they have dropped four more felonies on me. If you knew what I knew about the courts, that was definitely cause for concern, to say the very least.

## A SELF-INDUCED TORTUROUS HELL

But now I'm literally fighting for my life with heroin withdrawals. In my mind, my life was over as I knew it! The cold hard truth was that I was the loneliest, most desperate man on the planet at that point in my life. The hardest thing I have ever done in my life was writing this part of the book. The reason why is that I can now see how much I have changed since my arrest that night and how hopeless I truly was. I was standing there being booked in and a correctional officer at the jail looked at me and said, "You're gray. Are you ok?" They strip-searched me and dressed me in a black and white uniform. Then they put me into a holding cell. The door crashed behind me with a loud eerie bang and now I'm withdrawing from heroin! I didn't realize it then, but Satan was about to brutally assault me with demonic forces like I had never been assaulted before. He was about to push me to the brink of death and through the gates of darkness. It was very cold in my cell. I was lying there on the cold concrete bench. I was trying to sleep, but I couldn't. I woke up vomiting. I was trying my hardest to sleep, but now I'm six hours into withdrawing from heroin. When I woke up the next time, I was very weak and could barely walk. This time I have to use the toilet and I'm using the bathroom and throwing up in the same hole at the same time. It's not a pretty sight.

The nurse got there around six o'clock in the morning and she was a real sweetheart. She quickly explained that she couldn't give me any comfort medicine. That means suboxone, subutex, or methadone; these meds help with withdrawal symptoms. The nurse tells me that I am on my own. She checked my vital signs, and they were ok. But we had a major problem. She couldn't give me my insulin because I was shaking so violently from being cold. I could see the look on her face, and it was one of grave concern. She is worried about me but trying to play it off. The only problem was her hands were tied because of protocol.

They gave me a couple of blankets and a mat. Then put me back in my cell. At this point, I'm also starting to break down psychologically. The heroin withdrawals were a living hell. They are nothing like I could have ever dreamed of and they were also ten times worse than I could have imagined. They seemed to be induced by all the forces of Hell itself. As I'm lying there trying to sleep. I started losing control of all my bodily functions. I'm urinating, defecating, and throwing up all at the same time. I'm not trying to do it. It's just involuntarily. My mind is racing a million miles a second.

I sensed that presence of evil again. The same presence which was in the dream that night when I was twelve years old. I got a very eerie feeling and I could feel the hair stand up on the back of my neck. A thought was injected into my mind, "Your life is over." Then another thought was injected, "Your mom and dad are going to die while you're in prison." The condemnation continued as I heard, "You're such a horrible son. You made all that money and didn't even help your parents." My mind was beginning to race and I was instantly full of guilt, shame, condemnation, and remorse. I can see my mother and father. There was a feeling of dread in me that I couldn't describe to you if you gave me a lifetime. Then all of a sudden, that presence of evil that was with me in my truck that night, injected another thought into my mind and said, "You're a terrible father; you weren't even there for your children." A few minutes pass and another thought is injected into my mind. It says, "Your brother is going to die while you're in prison." I suddenly realize these are not my thoughts. I'm being tortured by demons. They are brutally assaulting me!

I tried to get up and make it to the toilet and I began to projectile vomit. I sit on the toilet as I throw up. I'm vomiting, defecating, and urinating so much that my stomach feels like someone tied a chain around it, hooked it up to a truck, and is trying to rip it out of me. I soon realized there was a war going on between good and evil. There is no doubt to me at this point. That it was for my soul! Mentally, physically, emotionally, and spiritually, I was being pushed to the brink of insanity and death! I could feel that the end was near. I wished for death because I felt so hopeless!

I then stumbled to the toilet to use the bathroom and suddenly I started to vomit. I couldn't hold it as I was sitting on the toilet. I tried to vomit in the hole while sitting on the toilet, and I vomited all down my chest. It was useless to fight this now, I know beyond a shadow of a doubt. I'm doomed! I felt like I was dying! I distinctly remember telling myself, "I wasn't going to die like this. That I had to fight, that if I was going to die, it wasn't going to be from heroin withdrawals. I had one young daughter who loved and adored me. I must not let my three daughter's Alice, Brenda, and Elaina remember me dying like this from heroin withdrawals." At that very moment, I thought of suicide. But I quickly ruled it out because I knew it would kill my mother and father. I stumbled back to my mat and just fell. I begged for mercy because I began urinating, defecating, and vomiting on myself on a regular basis. I didn't have the strength to make it to the toilet three feet away. It wasn't too long after that I realized I was all out of answers for the first time in my life.

I was lying there on the floor and I was as sick as you could possibly be. Let me remind you of something. I'm forty-one years old by number, going on 15. I can barely find the energy to wash my face. After two days, I finally slept for a couple of hours. I started dreaming about heroin. I was making a shot of heroin and I got it drawn up in the syringe. I'm about to put the needle in my vein, I sat straight up and vomitted everywhere. It was horrible because by this time there was nothing in my stomach to come up, but bile and mostly dry heaving. I haven't eaten anything in three days; I drink water to try to survive. But the only problem was that it would make me sicker and I would vomit, urinate, and defecate. I wished for death to come quicker.

The nurse and I later became good friends. She told me one day that she had never seen someone withdraw from heroin that badly. At one point, she even wondered if I would make it. But, there is one thing that never lies in the medical community: a person's vital signs. Mine were ok, time and time again.

## A LIFE-CHANGING PRAYER

I'm lying there on the floor of my cell. I'm on a mat and I'm a hot mess! My mind continues to race a million miles a second. Suddenly, it's almost as if, I'm in a dream. But I'm not. I start having flashbacks of my former life. My mind becomes like a movie, almost as if I'm in another time and another place. I'm in a semi-conscious state. Suddenly my life starts playing out in front of me, in my mind. I'm there with my first girlfriend and the mother of my two kids, Suzanne. I see her smile, it is a warm sunny day, and we're in a park in Haslet, Texas. She quickly disappeared. My third wife Nicki appeared and I saw her crying. There is a feeling of dread in me that can't be described in a million years. I saw my three daughters Alice, Brenda, and Elaina. I realize that they are sad. I saw my father and also I saw a lot of people whom I have hurt in one way or another. I saw my mother and I said to myself, "Oh thank goodness, everything will be alright; mom is here." Then the weirdest thing happened. In my mind's eye, I saw myself and I was five years old. I saw my mother kiss me on the cheek. I walked toward a

133

bus and it was a church bus! My mom sent me to church for the first time when I was five. Then I snapped back from the semi-conscious state that I was in and prayed the most sincere prayer I had ever prayed. I said, "God, please let me die."

At that point, I had lost all hope in self-righteousness! But then I saw the cross in my mind and there was Jesus Christ, the son of God, on it. I remembered there was a God and there was hope. I also remembered that he had all power and I could hear that old preacher man from way back in 1991. When I was at Buckner's Boys Ranch in Burnet, Texas, shout as if he was in the cell with me, "THERE'S HOPE AND VICTORY IN JESUS!"

Sadly at that moment, I remembered my relationship with my mother wasn't good. In retrospect, I unfairly blamed my mother for many things that went wrong in my life. But that experience, the one in that dream of her putting me on the church bus at five years old, would be the catalyst to get me to where I needed to be in eternity. It would be my mother's undying love and God's power that flowed to her and through her by way of the Holy Spirit, which would lead to my salvation on that day. I fell asleep that night and slept like a baby for the first time in days. I woke up on day five; I realized I had not only survived heroin withdrawals. But I came to the startling realization that I needed to get right with my Creator.

At that point, I was finally well enough to be housed with other inmates. They moved me later that day to the general population. I was housed with five other inmates. *I didn't know it then, but I had a newfound respect for my life and God's creation like I had never known.* I was still very sick, could barely sit up, and had to lean over while I sat down to watch television. I couldn't eat anything but one cookie at a time. I had no energy and was experiencing throat pain at the back of my mouth. I could eat Ramen noodle soup if it were cooked. I lost about ten pounds that first week. I was down to one hundred and forty-five pounds. I was forty pounds under my normal weight. My girlfriend back in Shreveport, Louisiana, was worried sick about me. She knew I was in jail, but she also knew I was very sick. She had a lot of unanswered questions. She didn't know I was wanted by the law, she didn't know I was a heroin addict, and she was completely perplexed by everything that was happening at the time. She saw me as a successful businessman and a great guy. I was good to her and we spent well over forty thousand dollars in just over two months. She had never been exposed to a real go-getter like I was. Simply put, I was an addict, and all addicts have these qualities. We all lead double lives; we are all pathological liars and master manipulators. That is exactly what I was and more.

## A GODLY SORROW THAT LEADS TO A TRUE REPENTANCE

It took me approximately thirty-five days to get back to normal from heroin addiction. In those thirty-five days, I began reading the Bible at least three to five times a day. Then one day, I was down in the dumps because I had just told my girlfriend back in Louisiana to go on without me and broke up with her. I began thinking about the future of my life. I got down on my knees and said, "God, I know you're real and I know I have done a lot of wrong in my life. Lord, I don't care what happens to me. I will accept full responsibility for my actions in this life and suffer the consequences. But please be the God of my life, glorify, honor, and praise yourself through me. Please Lord, Amen." You wouldn't believe it. As I got off that floor, it was like the weight of the world had been lifted off my shoulders. I was like a drowning man coming up for his first breath of air. The Creator and Sustainer of everything in existence. The one and only true God, had walked right through the walls of that fortress that I built around my heart as a twelve-year-old boy and carried out that scared little boy who was rejected by his father. It was almost as if He had told me himself, "I'll be your father; let me love you, you can trust me." I had a newfound respect for the Bible and the verse where God said, "I will never leave or forsake you." I can honestly say with all my heart, that my Heavenly Father has never let me down. God has blessed me exceedingly, abundantly, above and beyond, all I could ask, think, or imagine. The Bible says, that God will give you beauty for ashes and restore the years the locust have eaten. I can honestly say, "That we serve a God of restoration." The living God and the living hope!

# CHAPTER 7

---◆◆◇◆◆---

# SALVATION AND TRANSFORMATION

I began to learn how to have a relationship with God. I started to apply the word of God to my life. I quickly came to this startling realization. No matter what happened to me in my life, I had to agree with God's word. The reason was simple: I needed to recreate my life with the help of God. Since God was my creator. He knows what is best for me. I learned a scripture from the Bible that said, "Do not conform any longer to the patterns of this world but be TRANSFORMED by the renewing of your mind through the word of God. Then you will be able to know the acceptable, holy, pleasing, perfect will of God" (Romans 12:2). You see, I finally understood after all those years that I didn't need good advice like pep talks from other people. I needed the only advice that really matters in life: the great advice from the Bible. If I were going to have a true transformation and walk in victory, I would have to do what the word of God said, "The truly happy people are those who carefully study God's perfect law of liberty that makes people free, and they continue to study it. They do not forget what they heard, but they obey what God's teaching says. Those who do this will be made happy" (James 1:25). Bingo! That is what I had been searching for my whole life, to be loved, needed, wanted, and happy. But I never realized that fifty percent of our happiness is internal. I then began making myself stronger mentally, physically, emotionally, and spiritually. Through the living word, which is Jesus Christ (John 1:1). Jesus was the way I would rebuild my life. Jesus said, "I am the way, the truth, and the life, and no man shall come to the Father but by me" (John 14:6). After going through all that. I knew and believed my only hope was in God.

I realized very early on as a baby in Christ that there were three truths I had to live by to counter the lies of my former life. (1) Jesus, the way, the truth, and the life. (2) The gospel truth of the Bible, (3) and the Holy Spirit of Truth. That would give me a true transformation that would last a lifetime. I told you that I had been fighting everyone and everything my whole life! The world had taught me how to fight on to the bitter end. The world had taught me never to give up, no matter what was happening. But now, as Bill Wilson, the founder of Alcoholics Anonymous, had said in 1939, in the first edition of the A.A. "Big Book". *"We stood at the turning point, and we asked for his protection with complete abandon." What was I abandoning? That would be the complete abandonment of self. In the fourth edition of the A.A. "Big Book," Bill Wilson said, "Selfishness-self-centeredness! That, we think, is the root of our troubles. Driven by a hundred forms of fear, self-delusion, self-seeking, and self-pity, we step on the toes of our fellows, and they retaliate. Sometimes they hurt us, seemingly without provocation, but we invariably find that at some time in the past, we have made decisions based on self which later placed us in a position to be hurt. So our troubles, we think, are basically of our own making. They arise out of themselves, and the alcoholic or addict is an extreme example of a self-will run riot, though he or she usually doesn't think so. Above everything, we alcoholics and addicts must be rid of this selfishness. We must, or it kills us! God makes that possible, and there often seems no way of entirely getting rid of self without His aid. Many of us had moral and philosophical convictions galore, but we could not live up to them even though we would have liked to. Neither could we reduce our self-centeredness by wishing or trying on our own willpower. We had to have God's help."*

"This is the how and why of it. First of all, we had to quit playing God. It didn't work. Next, we decided that hereafter, in this drama of life, God was going to be our Director. He is the principal; we are his agents. He is the Father, and we are his children. Most good ideas are simple, and this concept was the keystone of the new triumphal arch through which we/I passed to freedom" (World Services, Inc. Staff, 1939). BINGO!" That statement by Bill Wilson, almost forty years before I was born, would describe me exactly. After reading the A.A. "Big Book," I realized for the first time in my life that I wasn't alone.

I layed there those four days in the torture chamber (holding cell), withdrawing from heroin. I was at the end of the road of self-sufficiency. My world of which I was the god of, and life as I knew it, was over. You see, at the end of the road to self-sufficiency. Which is exactly where I was at the time. The good Lord gives you a choice, just like he gave me that fateful day. You can fight on to the bitter end and go from a self-induced torturous hell you have created, or you can die and go to a place of weeping and gnashing of teeth, or you can choose to do what Jesus said, "If any man would come after me, he must deny himself and take up his cross and follow me daily" (Luke 9:23). I never dreamed when I begged God to let me die that day in that cell, that he would answer that prayer. But not in my wildest dreams did I ever anticipate that God would teach me that if I wanted to learn how to live life on life's terms, I would have to learn how to die to self, one day at a time. There must be total destruction of selfishness and self-centeredness! You must lose all hope in self-righteousness. In the Bible, Jesus said, "Those who want to save their lives will give up true life. But those who give up their lives for me will have true life" (Luke 9:24). Jesus said, "It is worth nothing for them to have the whole world if they themselves are destroyed or lost" (Luke 9:25). My whole life I was searching for a relationship with God through Jesus Christ because I needed that God-shaped void in my heart filled. The good Lord put that void in all of our hearts as an internal compass to point us to him for a relationship. That is what we're all created for. We all have interconnectedness. We are all like God in that sense. We are all relational beings, and to have good relationships, you must know how to love appropriately. I believe that in order to really know how to love correctly. You must do just like I did and find the author of unconditional love. That is Almighty God in three persons. The Father, Son, and the Holy Spirit.

I was still in a cell when I woke up on day five. I was in booking under twenty-four-hour observation. In other words, there were two officers that worked booking near me, and I was in a cell with a camera. Even though I was still sick, I was feeling better than I had been in the past. I had finally turned a corner and most of the withdrawal symptoms were gone.

They finally sent me back to the general population and I was housed in a cell with five other guys. I couldn't eat anything but Ramen noodle soup or cookies. The reason why was because I didn't have enough energy to chew my food and my throat hurt badly. I had to have a blanket on me twenty-four hours a day. I also had to sit down and bend over while I was sitting. I was in very bad shapeand I felt nauseated when I sat up straight. I was reading the Bible regularly though. Sadly, I lost almost ten pounds in the first week. I was emaciated and I was forty pounds underweight! I was grateful to be alive.

If I had a thousand lifetimes. I really truly believe that I could not find the words to describe the self-induced torturous hell I went through in that cell from every angle of my being that day. Mentally, physically, emotionally, and spiritually I was taxed to the max. I soon noticed that I had a newfound respect for life. I also realized how important people are for the first time in my life. It wasn't to long after this, I realized how much I needed relationships with other people. I never learned how to be interdependent with my family growing up. Again, I would like to reemphasize that I love my parents beyond comprehension. I would not change who my mother and father were for all the money on earth. They did the best they could with eight children and with the life skills they had. I also realized that after eighteen, I was no longer a victim of my upbringing. I was a volunteer in my own demise. After all those years, I finally accepted full responsibility for my actions. I conceded to the fact that I was at fault because I knew right from wrong. If I had struggled with that fact, I believe I would have forever bathed in the river of denial! Thank God I accepted that fact.

I started making my mind stronger by reading the Bible as much as possible. I believe that reading the Bible was very good Cognitive Behavioral Therapy for me. Then one day, I was sad and down in the dumps because I had to tell my girlfriend to move on without me. I knew right then it was just Jesus and me; that was all I had after forty-one years of life and apparently the writing was on the wall, Jesus was all that needed. I realized right then, that all we really have in this world is our relationship with God through Jesus Christ. There is no hope outside of Jesus Christ.

## THE BURDENS OF LIFE ARE REMOVED

I got down on my knees and said, "Lord, I know you're real. I have made a lot of mistakes in my life. I don't care what happens to me; I accept full responsibility for my actions, no matter what the circumstances or situation, and God I'm sorry for what I have done. Will you please take my life and glorify, honor, and praise yourself in and through me." I instantly felt the good Lord remove all my burdens from me. I got up off the floor, and it was as if someone had taken the weight of the world off my shoulders!

I started learning the scriptures. The most important part I learned is that I had to be sure I was not only a hearer of God's word. But more importantly, a doer. If not, I would definitely revert to my old behavior. You have probably heard it said a thousand times, "Nothing changes, if you don't change your thinking." That is a fundamental truth I would have to live by to stay sober one day at a time. The Bible says, "For though we walk in the flesh, we do not war according to the flesh. For the weapons of our warfare are not carnal but mighty in God for pulling down strongholds, casting down arguments. Every high thing that exalts itself against the knowledge of God, bringing every thought into captivity to the obedience of Christ and being ready to punish all disobedience when your obedience is fulfilled" (2 Corinthians 10:3-6). I live in this particular scripture today because we are all born with a reprobate mind which is hostile to God. Please allow me to dissect this particular scripture for you.

# BIBLICAL COGNITIVE SKILLS

Number one, if you hold every thought in captivity that exalts itself against the knowledge of God. This means you think about what you're thinking about. Number two, if something exalts itself against the knowledge of God, then it is a lie, because the word of God is the truth. If you act on that thought, you are not only outside God's will for your life, but you are living a lie! This is why it is so important that you renew your mind with the word of God. The Bible says, "We have the mind of Christ" (1 Corinthians 2:16). In the Bible, it also says, "In the beginning was the Word. The Word was with God, the Word was God, and He was with God in the beginning" (John 1:1). Jesus Christ is the living word. If you want true transformation, you must come to a Godly sorrow that leads to true repentance and salvation without regret. When I was twelve years old, my profession of faith was a sham because I confused repentance with regret. In other words, I regretted that I was a sinner. But that is only a step toward repentance in your heart and mind. If you repent, it means to turn around. In other words, convert to Christianity and turn from your sin. It means to repent of your sins from your heart, according to the Bible, by confessing with your mouth that Jesus Christ is Lord and believing in your heart that God raised him from the dead and you shall be saved (Romans 10:9). But you must continue to believe and repent one day at a time. You also must live a style of life by the narrow way of the Bible. This is all just by God's amazing saving grace through faith that we are able to do this. Then you get transformation through these three truths. The living word is Jesus. Jesus said, "I am the way, the truth, and the life. No man shall come to the Father but by me" (John 14:6). Remember what Romans 12:2 says, and I'm speaking out of context. It said,

"Do not conform any longer to the patterns of this world, but be TRANSFORMED by the renewing of your mind through the word of God." The last part of true repentance is by renewing your mind through the word of God. It is then that you can walk not after the flesh but after the spirit. If you think about it intently, it makes perfect sense. In other words, remember when I told you, God taught me that if I wanted to learn how to live my life, I would have to deny myself, take up my cross and follow him daily. What the Bible is saying is that I have to die to self and crucify my flesh. The Bible says, "The true children of God are those who let God's spirit lead them. The spirit we received does not make us a slave again to fear; it makes us children of God" (Romans 8:14-15). I told you earlier in another chapter that two things motivate a person to act how they do. Fear or faith! *Fear drives and motivates action, and faith leads and directs choice.*

My former life was all about me putting my faith in all the wrong places. In other words, I put my faith in my fear. I had a fear of being poor, so I put my faith in money. I chose to get my security from wealth, power, position, and prestige. These things are the world's measure of greatness. The god of this world Satan, robbed me of my identity in Christ at a very young age because he knew once he did that. I would have no power to overcome my sin problem. Satan knew that if he distracted me by crowning me with the riches of this world at a young age that I would get lost in the cares of life and be distracted from the will of God. Satan also knew then what I know now. That when that happens, you have lost your way in life. In other words, your Identity in Christ! Today, by God's grace, I know my identity in Christ. I know and believe beyond a shadow of a doubt that Christ is the source of my security. That Christ is the basis of my self-worth. I know beyond a shadow of a doubt that

"I am God's workmanship created in Christ Jesus to do good works which he prepared for me in advance" (Ephesians 2:10). I want you to know what I know now and that is this simple truth, you have eternal value. God loves you and wants a relationship with you. The living God and creator of all things is a sovereign Lord and in control of all things, at all times, in all creation. Almighty God breathed life into you. You and I are unique, special, and irreplaceable. There is no one on earth that has our D.N.A., Almighty God, the Creator of the universe, broke the mold when he made us. We are a masterpiece in God's eyes. We are the apple of God's eye. We are predestined for greatness. God knew when he created us that our future was so bright that we needed sunglasses! All the forces of Hell and even the Great Deceiver himself, Satan, couldn't stop God through Jesus Christ. Through the death, burial, resurrection, and ascension of Jesus Christ to the right hand of the Father is how Satan has become our defeated foe. I'm so thankful that we can come boldly to the throne of grace and know that Jesus Christ will make intercession for us, so that we can find grace and help in our time of need.

Satan doesn't want you to know what I know and believe. The word of God! The Bible says we have royal blood flowing through our veins as Christians. God has blessed, saved, sanctified, redeemed, justified, and delivered us. We as Christians have been transferred from the kingdom of darkness into God's kingdom. God's kingdom is a kingdom of light, righteousness, and truth. Satan's kingdom operates on fear, lies, and darkness and gives us sin, sickness, disease, and death.

God's kingdom gives us long life, eternal life, true life, and a life of abundance.

A life crowned with a sense of purpose that says, "I love you God and will you please use me to do your will and finish your work today?" A life that says, "No matter what happens in my life today. God I know you love me unconditionally and I trust you unconditionally Lord, because love always trusts." Furthermore, if you trust in God, "The joy of the Lord is your strength" (Nehemiah 8:10). Then you can truly rejoice and know what the Apostle Paul meant when he said, "Rejoice, rejoice in the Lord always. Let your gentleness be evident to all, for the Lord is at hand. Be anxious for nothing but by prayer and supplication, always with thanksgiving, submit your request to God, AND THE PEACE OF GOD WHICH SURPASSES ALL UNDERSTANDING WILL GUARD YOUR HEARTS AND MINDS IN CHRIST JESUS OUR LORD" (Philippians 4:4-8).

## PEACE WITH THE CREATOR

The solution to my sin problem as a person is peace with God through my faith in the Lord Jesus Christ. The solution and anecdote to addiction is also peace with God. When we are at peace with God, in our hearts and minds, we are ok with self and don't have to have all the false comforts that wreak havoc on our souls and cause premature death. You must realize something. If you live for the kingdom of darkness, those things happen to you. But, they happened for you if your Father is God and you serve him and God is truly the God of your life instead of a genie in a bottle whom you think is serving you. Let me ask you something. Does your faith serve you more than God and others? If you answered yes to that question. I want to encourage you to better your relationship with God. Also, you might be greatly deceived. That is dead faith at its best. That is exactly what I did for twenty-nine years. I used God to get what I could from him. I was never a follower of Christ. I was a fair weather fan. I never had any skin in the game. In other words, I never offered my body as a living sacrifice. I didn't love God enough to care what his will was for my life or others. Sadly, in the end, many people walked past me and went to their deaths. If I hadn't been so rebellious, many people could have come to know and believe in God through me. I am terribly sorry to my fellow man, God's creation, and my Creator for my selfishness. Today I realize that I'm God's creation, created to glorify him with my life. I realize this startling simple truth: all God wants is a relationship with me and more importantly, a relationship with you. He loves me and you so much that God sent his only son Jesus Christ to die for us while we were sinners, and this was not because we were good, but because the one matters.

After twenty-nine years, I finally realized and fully grasped the height, depth, width, and breadth of God's love for my fellow man and me. I think the Apostle Paul said it best, "Can anything separate us from the love Christ has for us? Can troubles, problems, suffering, hunger, nakedness, danger, or violent death? As it is written in the scriptures: For you, we are in danger of death all the time. People think we are worth no more than sheep being killed. But in all these things, we have full victory through God, who showed his love for us. Yes, I am sure that neither death, nor life, nor angels, nor ruling spirits, nothing know-nothing in the future, no powers, nothing in heaven, nothing in hell, nor anything else in the whole world will be able to separate us from the love of God that is in Christ Jesus our Lord" (Romans 8:35-39). I had been searching my whole life for the love of God in Christ Jesus. After all those years of self-induced torture. I had finally hit bottom and realized that I had a broken heart, and didn't know how to manage my life, and I WAS POWERLESS TO OVERCOME MY SIN PROBLEM. That was the absolute truth! It wasn't until I came to that startling realization that I could admit what the Apostle Paul said thousands of years before me to the church of Corinth. My brother in Christ, whom I have a lot in common with, had begged God to take away the thorn in his flesh. Although no one is sure of what the Apostle Paul's problem was. The third time God answered the Apostle Paul and said, "My grace is sufficient for you. My power is made perfect in weakness" (2 Corinthians 12:9). After reading this verse shortly after my conversion to Christianity. I realized right then in there, that I was weak in the flesh. But strong in the Lord and the power of his might. I truly believed for the first time in my life that I could do all things through Christ who strengthens me. I want to tell you something. God's grace was sufficient for me on that fateful day that I was lying in a holding cell at the Hancock County Jail, where my life was spent at forty-one years old.

## GOD'S GRACE IS SUFFICIENT FOR ME

But more importantly, I want to ask you, is God's grace sufficient for you? Let me ask you a question: was Jesus Christ being crucified on the cross at Calvary good enough for you to say to the living God and Creator of all things, "Your grace is sufficient for me, Lord?" The second question is, was the son of God's horrible death on the cross enough for you to say in faith, "Yes, Lord, I accept Jesus as my savior. I want you to be the only God of my life Jehovah. Please take your rightful place in my heart and life because you are worthy, Lord." That was basically what I had said to God approximately thirty-five days after I had gone through heroin withdrawal. I finally made it to the pages of the greatest book of all eternity, "The Lambs Book of Life." I had received the good Lord's grace through his son Jesus Christ.

The depths that God will go to in order to turn a sinner from the error of his way is unfathomable. The scriptures say, "Now the Lord is the Spirit, and where the Spirit of the Lord is, there is freedom" (2 Corinthians 3:17). Sadly, before I met Christ, the only freedom I had ever known was slavery. I was a slave to sin, a slave to things like my job, drugs, alcohol, money, power, position, prestige, sex, and success. But now that I'm a new creation in Christ Jesus. I'm a slave to righteousness because I'm the righteousness of God in Christ Jesus.

The greatest lesson I have ever learned from the Lord is how to love and cherish my relationship with him and my fellow man. The single most important factor in my life today is my relationship with God. After all those years of being and feeling enslaved, I finally got freed. It's almost as if I can hear Doctor Martin Luther King say, "*Free at last, I'm free at last. Thank God I'm free at last.*" Today I can truly say what Martin Luther King said before I was born. "Thank God I'm free at last."

There isn't a moment that goes by that I don't thank God for sparing my life. I realize God spared my life because He loves me and so that He can testify in and through me to his unconditional love, grace, mercy, compassion, and comfort to the whole world. Today I can truly say, "God is worthy!" I realized shortly after I said that prayer that day and surrendered my life to Christ. I received not only God's grace but also his unconditional love, mercy, compassion, and comfort. I then started to be a hearer and more importantly, a doer of God's word for the first time in my life. In other words, I surrendered my God-given free will and every detail of my life to the Lord daily. I kept reading the Bible and taking the best cognitive behavioral therapy you could get in the universe through the

Bible. I then kept applying God's word to my life. I kept doing what the scriptures said about continuing to work out my salvation with fear and trembling. Simply put, I became a doer of God's word, day in and day out. That made all the difference in the world. I kept believing, repenting, and living by the narrow way of the Bible daily. I also began to test and examine myself daily as the Bible talks about in thirty-one different scriptures. "Examine yourselves to see whether you are in the faith; test yourselves. Do you not realize that Christ Jesus is in you—unless, of course, you fail the test" (2 Corinthians 13:5)?

Martin Luther King said, *"Faith is not seeing the staircase, but taking the first step."* I realize looking back now, that I had very little faith, like Jesus had told people thousands of years before me. The Bible says, "Faith comes by hearing, and hearing the word of Christ" (Romans 10:17). In effect, it is simply saying faith comes by hearing the good news of the Bible, and people hear the good news when someone tells them about Christ. The Bible says, "Now faith is the substance of things hoped for, and evidence of things not yet seen" (Hebrews 11:1). The Bible also says, "By faith, we believe that those things which are seen, we're formed by which we can't see" (Hebrews 11:3). Furthermore it says, "Without faith, it is impossible to please God because anyone who comes to God must believe that he is, and he is a rewarder of those who diligently seek him" (Hebrews 11:6).

I realized as a baby in my walk with Christ that my entire walk as a Christian would have to be by faith. If not, I couldn't please God. Another startling realization I came to was that if I was going to please God, I would have to walk by faith and not by sight. Do you remember when I told you about the curse of the law of sin and death? I told you about another law in the Bible that says, "Through Christ Jesus, the law of the spirit that brings life made me free from the law that brings sin and death" (Romans 8:2). The truth of the law of the spirit of life is exalted in our bodies when we surrender our free will to God through Jesus Christ, including every thought, emotion, attitude, and behavior. By doing so, we can truly speak the truth about ourselves, as stated in the scriptures. God is in us acting according to his will and good pleasure.

## CLAIM YOUR VICTORY

Remember, the victory is already yours. Jesus Christ bought and paid for it all. It is a gift from God. But we must claim our free gift from God for all of our eternity through Jesus Christ. We must do this by believing not only in Jesus Christ, but by believing we can do all things through Christ who strengthens us. Salvation is by faith and faith alone in Jesus Christ. It is preceded and followed by repentance. We must also believe that it is not by our own might, not by our own power, but by God's Spirit. Salvation is a supernatural work of God. My friend, I beg you to come out of the pain, let go, and allow God to give you true life, eternal life, joy, peace, contentment, and a life crowned with a sense of purpose. More importantly, let God give you your passion back, let God give you your zest for life back, let God through Christ Jesus light that eternal flame in your heart, let him stir your spirit, let him show you how gifted, talented, well abled, and thoroughly equipped you are.

Remember this as long as you live. You might be down, but you're not out. God has the final say so in your life. You might be lonely, but at just the right time, God will bring you the right person, and he or she will be twice as good as that person or persons that walked out on you. You may not have the greatest cognitive behavior. In other words, great cognitive behavior is Godly thinking, a renewed mind through the word of God, but you can have it really easy with your willingness to change. We must do our part and put forth the effort to have a great relationship with God.

You might not have seen a dream come to pass; it might be taking longer than you thought. You might feel like the world has forgotten about you, but Almighty God loves you and has you right in the palm of his hand and even though you have made some mistakes, always remember that the living God and Creator of all things is in control of your life and you will fulfill your God-given destiny. The medical report might not be good. But instead of believing the lies of Satan, you must say to yourself in faith, "God promised the number of my days He will fulfill." The child you're having trouble with, don't walk away from them; keep speaking those positive faith filled words over them like the book of Joshua in the Bible says, "But if serving the LORD seems undesirable to you, then choose for yourselves this day whom you will serve, whether the gods your ancestors served beyond the Euphrates or the gods of the Amorites, in whose land you are living. But as for me and my household, we will serve the LORD" (Joshua 24:15). God is opening up doors for you that no one can shut. He is closing the doors you don't need open. He has given you divine health, prosperity, connections, divine opportunities, renewing of the mind, recovery, transformation, healing, health, and wholeness through the Lord Jesus Christ. The great thing is that to top all of that off. God has blessed you exceedingly and abundantly, above and beyond, all you can ask, think, or imagine!

God has promised you beauty for ashes. God is your vindicator. My point to all this is that if you put your faith in a defeated mentality in your natural carnal, earthly, sinful mind, things happen to you. But if you renew your mind with the scriptures then you will not only get transformation. But because you have the mind of Christ. You will confess, believe, and receive God's promises over your life and the life of those around you. The reason why is very simple. You will be walking by faith and not by sight. In order for you to walk in victor, you have got to walk by faith. Then you will begin to call things that are not as though they are out of faith. It is then that you will begin to believe what Almighty God says about your life and you will stop believing the lies of the enemy. If you will speak God's word over your life and those around you.I believe and declare in the mighty name of Jesus, you will come to the fullness of your God-given destiny.

## MUNGER'S POSITIVE, UPLIFTING, FAITH-FILLED WORDS

I want to tell you about the impact you can make on someone's life by speaking positive, faith-filled words over them. In 2018, I was fortunate to meet a man named Dan Munger, a great man of faith. I had just got arrested and to the Hancock County Jail. So obviously, nobody knew me there, and I was a stranger. But God put favor in the heart of Dan Munger towards me. Something happened in a pod where I was housed. I didn't know it at the time. But Dan was talking to Warden Brandon Zeringue a couple of days before the incident had occurred. Dan spoke positive, faith-filled words, over my life while he was speaking to the Warden that day. Dan simply told the Warden that I was an honest man, which was crazy to me at the time. I had been called everything but an honest man and was in jail for being dishonest. But Dan Munger, a friend who sticks closer than a brother, applied this principle and called things that were not, as though they were, out of good faith. He didn't call me by my sin. Dan spoke those positive faith-filled words over my life to the Warden of the Hancock County Jail.

I didn't know it at the time. But one day, they called me out for medical. Then they walked me to the Warden's office. It was the Warden, Captain, and Sergeant. As I walked in, I thought this definitely was not good. Warden Brandon Zeringue looked straight at me and said, "Dan Munger tells me you're an honest man." I nodded my head. He asked me a question about a fight I knew nothing about. I asked him, "How come he didn't roll the cameras back?" He dismissed me after a few moments. But something happened to me as I walked back to the pod where I was housed at. I felt something deep down inside of me say, "Honest man?" Wow! I had been called a lot of things in my lifetime. I've got to tell you, I had never been called an honest man! I had been called everything but an honest man!

Something happened to me that day when he spoke those positive, faith-filled words over my life. It was as if God had just used a human being to inject and birth honesty in me! Coincidentally, shortly after that, Chaplain Dan Munger. A former Commander in the United States Navy who fought for his country in the Iraq war. Dan started an in-house rehab at the Hancock County Jail under Sheriff Ricky Adam's administration. The next thing you know, I'm the first candidate on the list to go.

On page 58 of the fourth edition of the Alcoholics Anonymous "Big Book," it is titled "How It Works" (Services, 2007). H.O.W. is an acronym for honesty, open-mindedness, and willingness. It said, "Rarely have we seen a person fail who has thoroughly followed our path. Those who do not recover cannot or will not give themselves to this simple program—

USUALLY, MEN AND WOMEN WHO ARE CONSTITUTIONALLY INCAPABLE OF BEING HONEST WITH THEMSELVES." I stress the honest part. I soon realized that without honesty in recovery the power of self-deception takes effect and you live in the river of denial. That was not only God preparing me to recover through Dan Munger and Warden Brandon Zeringue speaking positive faith-filled words over my life. But the good Lord knew I needed to be honest to fully recover from the disease of addiction.

God then used Dan Munger and the Warden to get me where I needed to be to change my life. That is exactly how the good Lord works. God at that moment was preparing me to not only get clean and sober. But he was also preparing me to fulfill my God-given destiny. Which by the way is greatness; however he sees fit as the God of my life to glorify himself in and through me, to all of humanity is perfectly fine with me. I had someone ask me one time what this book was about. I told them it was God's story about my life. I simply told that person that Almighty God is the author of this book, and every life is a story, and every story matters. People have asked me if the book will be published. I simply tell them I'm already a published author in God's kingdom. But no doubt it will be. In other words, this book is not about me any more than my life is about me. The Bible says, "For to me to live is Christ, to die is gain" (Philippians 1:21). This book is about God glorifying himself through a former liar, cheat, thief, con, swindler, alcoholic, drug addict, and master manipulator who woke up at 41 years old and succumb to the startling realization that his former life was all a huge lie, and that he had been reduced to a life of mediocrity and a one cell radius.

This book is about a man who once was lost, but now he is found, about a man that was blind. But God in all his saving grace, has now allowed him to see the error of his ways. I'm certain you can see that I made a fatal mistake in my former life. That hurt a lot of people and almost cost me my life. I made it all about me. I want to ask you an honest question. Is your life about glorifying yourself and satisfying yourself more than God or helping your fellow man? I promise you that you can never fulfill your God-given destiny thinking like that.

Why would you settle for less and rob God of the glory in your life because of selfishness? Why not live your best life now by surrendering your life to Christ? Why don't you trust God to bless you exceedingly, abundantly, above and beyond all you can ask, think, or imagine? Do you say you love the Lord? If so, "Love always trusts" (1st Corinthians 13:7). In other words, what I'm trying to get you to see here is if you're just giving God lip service or not. Do you honestly believe that God is truly the God of your life? In other words, are you continuing to work out your salvation with fear and trembling? Do you believe that your faith is being perfected by your works through the virtuous promptings of the Holy Spirit? Can you see the fruits of the Spirit in your life from the Lord? Are you testing and examining yourself daily to see if you're in the faith? If you answered no to any of those questions, which are between God and you. I strongly encourage you to ask God to help you work on your relationship with him because He is worthy! That is the pure motive of the heart God looks at. Please don't be like me in my former life and out of ignorance, think a better resume can get you to Heaven. Don't say and do things so you can go to Heaven or so that you will not burn in Hell. But because God is worthy.

More importantly, do it so others may live a life of victory and have an abundant life. Do it so God can love and help others through you! In my former life, I measured greatness by what people thought of me, how much money I had and by how many women I slept with. I'm sure you understand what I'm saying, by everything that doesn't matter. But when I woke up half dead from heroin withdrawals, my life was spent at forty-one years old. God in all his mercy, reached down and touched my heart with his love, grace, and compassion. It was then that I realized the most important thing in life, is my relationship with the Lord and his creation. The reason being is very simple: that is what is important to my Heavenly Father; that is why He sent his son Jesus Christ to die for me and more importantly for you, my dear friend.

I want to tell you a story about Reverend Richard Wurmbrand. This man wrote a book called "Tortured for Christ." He tells the story in the 1960s about living in communist Romania. This is his account of the communist and secret police who tortured him for being a Christian after his release from prison in 1965. This man was tortured in prison for fourteen years just for being a Christian. Richard said, *"Shortly before he was released to go to the United States, the secret police warned him never to speak about his torture. He stated the communist regime had great confidence in the brainwashing through which he passed. In the West, there are now many who have passed through the same things as Richard did but who remained silent for good reason. Some of even praised communism after having been tortured by the Communists. The Communists were very sure that Richard, too, would be silent."*

*So, in Richard's words, this is what he said, "In December of 1965, my family and I were allowed to leave Romania. My last deed before leaving was to go to the grave of the colonel who had given the order for my arrest and who had ordered my years of torture. I placed a flower on his grave. By doing this, I dedicated myself to bringing the joys of Christ that I have experienced to the Communists, who are so empty spiritually. I hate the Communist system, but I love the men. I hate the sin, but I love the sinner. I love the Communists with all my heart. Communists could kill Romanian Christians, but they couldn't kill the Christian love toward even those who tortured and killed them. I have not the slightest bitterness or resentment against the Communist or my torturers* (Wurmbrand, 1974)."

My friend, that is a powerful testimony of the love of God in Christ Jesus. The Bible says, "Love carries no record of wrongs" (1 Corinthians 13:5). Furthermore, the Bible says, "By this everyone will know that you are my disciples if you love one another" (John 13:35). Look at the word bitterness on that last line from Richard Wurmbrand's statement. One definition of bitterness is carrying a record of wrongs. When Jesus was on the Cross, He looked down at the people he came to die for who had just brutally murdered Him with the worst death possible and said, "Father forgive them, for they know not what they do."

You can kill the Christian, but you can't kill love. The reason why is very simple. The Bible says, "God is Love" (1st John 4:8,16). You can't kill God, my friend. I'm so grateful that God made me a new creation and gave me true transformation. I know and believe that I got it through my relationship with God through Jesus Christ, and because of this, I can give someone else the gift that keeps on giving. I'm also grateful that I can glorify God with my life in this manner, even after I'm dead and gone. What I give to others, especially Christ will live on forever. Every time I think of that, I just smile and say, "God, you are awesome." That my friend is the love of God in Christ Jesus at work in humanity today.

# MY DYING WISH

My only wish when I leave this world is that I will leave behind a Godly legacy. I thank my Father who has made that possible through his son Jesus Christ, for I know this is my reasonable service. Today, by God's grace, in the same manner, that Author Richard Wurmbrand had a heart of compassion for his Communist torturers. I too, have a heart of compassion when I look at humanity these days.

Someone once asked me, "Why bother to help addicts? It is a heart-wrenching business?" I told them that when my life was over at the ripe old age of forty-one years old, God in all his love, grace, and mercy, reached out and turned my heart of stone into a heart of compassion and it was all to his glory. I'm eternally grateful today in my actions and since I share a common peril with addicts, why would I not share my experience, strength, and hope with God's creation? I must say, "That it is a true honor to be used by God in this manner." I don't believe in coincidences! But coincidentally, love is a person, it is God, and Love is shown in action (1st Corinthians 13:4-8). God is Love and is in me, prompting me, to act according to his will and good pleasure. Therefore any time I can share my experience, strength, and hope in this life with my fellow man and help them in any way. It is my duty, honor, and privilege to be able to do so.

As I sat in the Hancock County Jail awaiting a felony indictment on multiple gun and drug charges. I realized somehow, the good Lord was going to get me out of all this trouble. I have known and believed from day one that He will do it according to his will for my life. I decided to attend Alcoholics Anonymous meetings at the jail two times a week.

One day as I was working out in the dayroom, waiting to attend an A.A. meeting. I felt the Holy Spirit impress upon my heart to make sure that I was the last one out the door that day. This thought became ingrained in my mind rather quickly. I thought ok, I got plenty of money and coffee, so I don't mind going last. My motive for going was not for coffee. But some other guys weren't as fortunate as I was to have enough money on their books to afford coffee from the canteen. It wasn't too long after the first prompting that I once more was prompted again by God's Holy Spirit to be the last one out the door. I went back to working out and then the door flung open, and Chaplain Dan Munger yelled, "A.A." I looked around and started to step out the door. But as I looked back there was a straggler that was still coming to the door. I stepped inside the door and said, "Brother, you go ahead of me." Dan looked at me intently and said, "That was very kind of you, but that is all we have enough room for today." Then Dan looked at me and said, "I will make sure you go the next time." Even though I didn't get to go to a meeting that day, that simple act of obedience would spark a lifelong relationship between Dan Munger and I.

## CHAINBREAKER'S REHABILITATION PROGRAM

Afterwards I was allowed to attend A.A. meetings every time, with no problems. Not long after that, Chaplain Dan Munger started his one-of-a-kind "Chainbreakers" in-house drug and alcohol treatment program. I was honored enough to be in the first class. The first night I had eight hours of homework. I finally finished and said to myself, "Dan is crazy if he thinks I'm going to keep doing this every night." I had always disliked writing. I just never had the patience for it. I changed my attitude, though. I finished the class, I made like a 99 average and went on to be the valedictorian of the first "Chainbreakers" class. I believe I had two incorrect answers out of about three hundred questions during the entirety of the course.

At the graduation, Sheriff Ricky Adam, Warden Brandon Zeringue, and the Honorable Judge Hoda were there with all the men's families in the courtroom. I was asked to speak to the men and their families by Chaplain Dan about the Biology of Addiction. I accepted the offer and said, "Well, I've sold approximately $22,000,000-$25,000,000 dollars worth of roofing in my lifetime, so I guess I could speak to a few strangers for ten minutes about the disease of addiction with no problem."

I spoke about the Biology of Addiction. Then in my final words, I said, "I want to ask you all a question. If you had five minutes to live, what would be important to you? Would you call for your plane and get that G650 Gulfstream rocking at thirty-thousand feet? Would you get your one hundred thousand dollar diamond-encrusted Rolex watch out and look at it one more time? Would you call your financial consultant and say come on over and let me look at my portfolio one last time?" I said, "Let me tell you what would be important to me at that moment. It would be my relationship with God and others." I then said, "If I had five minutes to live and one thing to say to you outside of, 'I love you,' I would tell you what the Apostle Paul told folks two thousand years ago, 'Forget those things which are behind, and press toward the mark for the high calling of God in Christ Jesus' (Philippians 3: 13-14). Never forget these two things! God is real, people are God's creation, and they are what matters most."

# A MESSAGE FROM MY FATHER IN HEAVEN

The ceremony was over and as everyone was visiting with their families. There was an older gentleman that came up to me and said, "Son, what did you say you did for a living? I think you just found your calling." That was it! I sincerely believe God was preparing me all those years while I was selling roofing to do his will and finish his work, to further his kingdom, by witnessing to people everywhere and demonstrating his goodness. But if I had not listened to the Holy Spirit's virtuous promptings that day and waited to go to "A.A.," I don't know where I would be today. I owe my life to God through Jesus Christ my Lord. I also realize that if it wasn't for the measure of Dan Munger's surrender and God acting in him according to his will and good pleasure. I would still be living in utter hopelessness and despair in active addiction. The point of all this is for the first time in my life. I had stepped outside myself and started helping others. In turn, I began reaping what I had sowed. I'm so grateful to God, Dan, and Joan Munger for saving me from imminent death. I was as good as dead in those last days of my former life. As graduation ended, I realized I had to keep surrendering my life to God, through Jesus Christ, one day at a time.

Shortly after graduation, I was still in the general population and started doing Alcoholics Anonymous meetings in the pod, where I was housed. There was a great response from the inmates every time I held a meeting in my cell. It not only helped me from a peer support group standpoint. But more importantly, God taught me a very valuable lesson about life by doing the A.A. meetings. I learned that anytime on this side of Heaven, that I can add value to another human life, especially an addict's life, that it is my duty as a Christian to bring hope and love to a dying world.

I was talking to Dan Munger one day and was telling him my life story. I could see the look on his face when I looked up at him. He knew that I had a long road ahead of me. I believe wholeheartedly that he knew that I needed a miracle and it would depend on four things if I got it or not. My ability to be rigorously honest with myself and others, open-mindedness to change cognitively, my willingness to insert the word of God in my life, which brings true transformation, and last but not least, my willingness to go to any length to surrender my God-given free will in every detail of my life back to the Creator and Sustainer of life.

## WATCHING THE TRUE FOLLOWERS OF CHRIST CLOSELY

When Dan looked up at me, I could tell he choosing his words very carefully, always letting his conversation be seasoned with grace. He said, "The only way to counter your former life of selfishness and self-centeredness is to live a life of self-giving." Bingo! Right then and there, I quickly accepted that startling realization. I knew the former Navy Commander had wrestled with his own demons when he was a young man, not quite like mine. But he had come back from being as dead as a man in the grave himself. Although I must say, "Dan was a much better man on his worst day than I was on my best day in my former life." Dan was seventy years old and a fine specimen of a genuine Christian, with a genuine love for all of humanity, because he had learned a man reaps what he sows. Dan also knew that people were God's creation and that was what really mattered in life. He knew what I chose to be ignorant of and that was the startling truth that we all have interconnectedness. We are all relational beings, made in God's image. Dan also knew that all my hurts came from broken relationships and all my healing would come from God through the healthy relationships I created. Obviously, with the help of the Lord. But there was a key factor that needed bolstering. I would have to get my relationship right with the Lord first. Then he would use people, especially those acting according to his will and good pleasure, to heal me completely, one day at a time, while I did my part and depended on him.

So, I closely watched every move my good friends Dan and Joan Munger made at the Hancock County Jail. I watched everything they did and began to see the Lord at work in humanity through my newfound friends. I saw how they responded appropriately to very unlovely creatures like me, addicts, and criminals. I watched my good friend and his wife die to self, so that God's Holy Spirit could be exalted in their bodies. I realized that the good Lord could love his creation back from the depths of the grave through genuine Christians or however He saw fit. I saw God doing what I'm telling you. I literally came to know the true meaning of "Love conquers all." My friends were helping countless people in their community daily inside and outside the Hancock County Jail.

I watched them give endlessly day after day of what the good Lord had given them. They gave of their time, talents, works, and possessions. But the most important thing I saw was them laying down their lives for their friend Jesus and their fellow man. The Bible says, "Greater love hath no man than this, that a man lay down his life for his friends" (John 15:13, KJV). They were loving people unconditionally because God is in them. I couldn't figure it out at first. I thought there had to be something that they were getting. But I couldn't have been more wrong. They were the best human beings I had ever encountered in my lifetime. I suddenly realized that the good Lord had strategically placed them in my life. I was shocked when I figured out that God was at work in humanity through Dan and Joan Munger and all my brothers and sisters in Christ around the world. I could see God's Holy Spirit at work in humanity for the first time in my life because I was redeemed. I was a child of the one and only true God. I had true hope and it came from the Living Hope, Almighty God. I realized how fortunate I was to be alive and also how fortunate I was to be a Christian. I was grateful that my Heavenly Father was using me to do his bidding. I was alive and for the first time in my life, all was well with my soul; no matter what happened to me, I knew that I could truly say, "All is well with my soul Lord." I recognized that when I was near death in my former life, God had resurrected me from not only a physical death but also from a spiritual death! About six months later, all of the money I came into jail with was spent on canteen. Then I was broke, hungry, and sitting in jail. I was stuck wondering how I was going to buy hygiene products. But I was still praising the Lord, doing his work, and grateful to be alive.

## THE RIGHT THING IS THE ONLY THING

I knew that I couldn't go back to being a bookie in prison or selling tobacco or drugs, so I said to myself one day, "I would rather be hungry and right in the eyes of my maker, pleasing God out of faith, than to be a stumbling block to my fellow man another minute." I prayed to God one day and said, "Please, let me become an inmate worker. So I could get extra food and have something constructive to do with my time besides working out all day." You wouldn't believe what happened next. I'm diabetic, so I stepped into the hallway to go to medical and check my blood sugar a couple of days later and you're not going to believe this! I looked up and saw Warden Brandon Zeringue standing at the desk where the officers conduct business. He looked straight at me and then back down at a sheet of paper. Then Warden Zeringue looked up again and said, "O'Dell, you're moving to the inmate worker pod today." I couldn't believe God had pulled that off. I have not been an inmate worker in almost twenty years. My point is that our Heavenly Father knows exactly what we need and when. We must believe that God has supplied all of our needs according to his riches and glory in Christ Jesus. God also can put favor in the hearts of men and women that you couldn't earn in a thousand lifetimes to help you get to your God-given destiny. Just like He did with Warden Zeringue for me that day.

The Bible says, "The King's heart is in the hands of the Lord, like the rivers of water; He turns it wherever He wishes" (Proverbs 21:1). Later that day, I was moved to the inmate worker pod and I became the jail librarian. The job took a couple of hours a week. But the good Lord had a plan. I started helping clean the hallway, medical, booking, Justice Court, administration side, and the shop, where I serviced the patrol cars under a master mechanic who worked for the Hancock County Sheriff's Office. I was honored they would put enough faith in me to work on their vehicles. I got all those jobs through my work ethic created years earlier in the roofing business and God's favor. I started working seventeen hours a day, seven days a week. Then I would teach an advanced theology course watered down to an eighth-grade level when I finished work. I

166

became well-known for my work ethic, integrity, character, and my love for the Lord.

Then one day, not long after that, Dan asked me to start teaching the "Chainbreakers" rehabilitation program to the inmate workers. I jumped at the opportunity to help my fellow man. But you have to understand something. After you work seventeen hours a day, it is very difficult to capture the attention of an addict for three hours. The hard part is that I would have to teach at least one of those hours. But be there three hours regardless, because this rehab is recognized by the Circuit Court. You wouldn't believe it! God gave me the gift of teaching. Looking back now, I understand completely, that when you honor the Lord, he will honor you back. The reason why is simple, because he knows you will give all the glory to him. I was so thankful to be able to give back the same thing to these men that I was so freely given, which was a life I had never known. A life of sobriety of course. But true life, abundant life, eternal life, a life of meaning and purpose, that was so much bigger than me. Then on top of all that. I was glorifying God with my life. I must say, "The Holy Spirit is powerful." I have been fortunate enough to speak to High School kids, at treatment centers outside of the Hancock County Jail, multiple churches, teach Bible courses at the jail twice a week, and teach "Chainbreakers" every other month for thirty days straight. I did it all by God's grace and to his glory! It is amazing to me to look out at an audience, speak to them about my life story, and watch the Holy Spirit move across the room and touch the hearts and minds of the men and women in the room. God is awesome. I'm so thankful to be used by God to fulfill his purposes. We have graduated over five hundred men and women from "Chainbreakers" since it started in 2019 at the

Hancock County Jail. There is a thirty to sixty percent success rate.

A lot of times that I speak, the audience is so moved that people are in tears. It has truly been an honor to testify to God's goodness in my life and to speak the same positive faith-filled words over the lives of people that were spoken over me by total strangers who believed in me in my darkest hour—even when I didn't believe in myself anymore. We serve a God who is always right on time. There is no doubt that God is real! I AM LIVING PROOF! I was hopeless. But God in Christ Jesus, rich in mercy, gave me beauty for the ashes that I had made of my life through the hope and victory that only comes with having a relationship with God through his son Jesus Christ. I always teach my students how to make this triumphal arch of freedom with the twelve steps of Alcoholics Anonymous so they can walk right through it and meet God through his son Jesus Christ. True freedom only comes from God because we're all slaves to sin! Today I say, "Free at last, I'm free at last. Thank you, God. I can finally help someone else be free at last because I have true freedom in Christ!" I realize my life is not about me anymore. But my life is about my relationship with God bringing hope and love to a dying world through Jesus Christ.

I began walking with the Lord. One day at a time, I began to surround myself with strong men and women of faith. These were the people I kept closest to me. My inner circle, so to speak. These were genuine Christians with a genuine love for all of humanity. These great men and women of faith were Dan and Joan Munger, Pat Burke, Jay and Rhonda Gamble, and Tony. I watched them very closely.

I viewed Almighty God's grace flow freely to and through these men and women, to everyone around them. It was then that I saw God in them acting according to his will and good pleasure for the first time in my life. I could recognize God in humanity at work; it was a beautiful vision.

It wasn't long after that I began to recognize God speaking to me. I realized suddenly that God's voice was the one I heard in church that day when I was twelve years old. I studied the Bible intently without accepting any hollow philosophies and doctrines of men into my spirit. I started to receive the mind of Christ, realizing, knowing, and believing that what the scriptures said about me is my truth and what I believe about me and others. I began to have a Christian worldview.

The Bible says, "If any man be in Christ, he is a new creation" (2nd Cor. 5:17). The good Lord helped me take off every negative label I put on myself when I served the god of money and Satan's purposes. I went from being an alcoholic, drug addict, liar, cheat, thief, con, adulterer, fornicator, untrustworthy, unreliable, and master manipulator with no character or integrity. By the grace of God, I became a child of the Most High God, created in Christ Jesus to do good works, which he prepared for me in advance. I was a new creature and exhibited the fruits of the Spirit in my life to prove it.

I continued to work out my salvation with fear and trembling. In other words, I was walking my faith out. I kept testing and examining myself as the Bible talks about in thirty-one different scriptures. I was doing all the right things because that was the only thing I could do. I was loving God in truth and action. In other words, after all those bad choices, I learned I would do the right thing every time. The reason why was really simple. My days of doing the wrong thing were over.

Then the inevitable finally happened. I was indicted on felony gun and drug charges after 15 months and then the state of Mississippi handed me a habitual indictment. It was a three-count indictment with an enhancement on all of the charges, which made me eligible for twice the punishment.

## FACING 56 MANDATORY YEARS IN PRISON

As I look back now, I can remember it like it was yesterday. My Attorney walked into the visiting room one day before court, and he said, "Mr. O'Dell, on count one, you are facing twenty mandatory years day for day, without the eligibility for parole. On count two, you're facing twenty mandatory years day for day, without the possibility of parole. On count three, you're facing sixteen years day for day. You're staring down the barrel of a total of 56 mandatory years day for day in prison."

I was stunned! I suddenly felt like I was gonna faint. My attorney then looked at me and said, "Son, someone in this town has written multiple letters to the judge on your behalf. If it weren't for them, you would be in a world of trouble. You should find out who it is and thank them. The District Attorney's office has made you an offer of five years day for day. I can probably get them down to three."

I could suddenly breathe again. I told my attorney I would take the five instead of the three because I had a ministry here at the jail and something deep down in my spirit told me to stay here. I was probably going to do time in Texas anyway and my time here would most likely count there. I listened to the Lord and trusted in him with all of my heart.

Then a couple of months later at the height of Covid-19, my mother called me at Christmas and said, "Son, your father isn't doing well and he wanted me to tell you he would like to talk to you." I spoke to my father and he was doing horrible. I told him

I loved him as he was in tears over the phone. My mother got back on the phone and was hysterical and said, "Son, I don't know what I'm going to do if your dad dies." I said, "Mom, I love you and everything will be ok."

Approximately one month later, Lieutenant Andrew Johnson, a man who had almost fourteen years with the Hancock County Sheriff's Office. Mr. Johnson rose through the ranks from being a correctional officer to being the Assistant Warden in 2021. I witnessed Lieutenant Johnson at the time start walking from master control toward medical. I was standing by the laundry room. Lieutenant Johnson and I were pretty close because I spent all my time working around him and the other staff members at the jail. So naturally you get to know the staff really well.

I remember it like it was yesterday. I saw Lieutenant Johnson who at that time had not yet made the rank of Captain. He was walking down the hallway. I saw him stop the Warden with a piece of paper in his hand. All my friends from the Chaplain's office were locked out of the jail because of Covid-19. I watched Johnson say something to the Warden and I could tell it was bad. Then Warden Brandon Zeringue quickly looked back at me. I could see it was really bad in his eyes when he looked at me. The Warden shook his head and instructed his top Lieutenant to do something. Lieutenant Andrew Johnson turned and said, "Follow me, O'Dell." Lieutenant Johnson took me to the back dock of the jail. He then looked at me with a somber look and said, "Your sister Tammie O'Dell just called; your mother Emma has died." That was the worst thing that could have happened to me. I was shaken to the core of my being. I was crushed! I had never had a family member close to me die. I was a momma's boy and now my mom is gone forever. I was instantly full of guilt, shame, and condemnation! All I could think of was my mother's last thoughts of me being locked up and how I robbed my mother of at least 15 years of my life by being locked up.

I called home to my sister and they dropped another bombshell on me. My sister told me that it was a suspected suicide. She told me it would be a while before they could get the toxicology report from the Coroner's Office because of Covid-19! It was a one-two-knockout punch straight to my heart that rocked me harder than Mike Tyson rocked boxers in the early 1990s! I walked outside and got down on my knees. I prayed for God to help me get through my mother's death. I had to preach a sermon the next morning. I knew and believed God was still on the throne.

The next morning I got up, and I felt an indescribable emptiness deep inside of me. It hurt me to lose my mother with a pain I wouldn't wish on anyone. I walked into the kitchen like I had so many other mornings and all the lights were off. I turned the lights on and when I saw the stainless steel tables in my mind, I could picture my mother on one of those stainless steel tables in the morgue, cold and all alone. I almost collapsed. But I was being held up by a table. I prayed, "God help me, your servant." I quoted a scripture that came to mind that the Lord Jesus said, "To all you who are heavy laden, cast your burdens upon me, for my yoke is easy and my burden is light" (Matthew 11:28-30). I asked God to take that burden from me. I was hurt worse than you can imagine, but the suicide part almost killed me. You can never imagine the pain I felt in my heart.

I went down to the classroom later that morning. The classrooms are in the back of the Hancock County Jail. I did this like I had done countless times before. I got to the classroom full of men and preached a sermon on the love of God in Christ Jesus that Billy Graham would have been proud of. There wasn't a dry eye in the room. By the grace of God, it was a powerful sermon.

I told the men at the end of the sermon, not to be like me and wait to change their lives when it was too late. What I meant by that was they shouldn't wait until their loved ones are gone forever. I asked them not to waste another minute of their lives on self. Then I instructed them to go home and love their families while they helped others. I didn't want to preach that day because I was hurting. But deep down inside, I knew the good Lord was still on the throne and all this was preparing me to help minister to someone else in the future who had lost a loved one. The good thing was that now I could identify with how someone felt that had lost a loved one by personal experience. Although the enemy of our souls, Satan, tried to use it as a stumbling block. I knew that God would make it right in the end and it would be a stepping stone to making me stronger. I knew then and believe now that it would help me fulfill my God-given destiny.

I knew my older brother Brandon was battling stage 3 liver cancer and not doing well. A few weeks before my mother's death, my family had called me and told me my brother was in the hospital and wasn't expected to make it through the night. My mother called the jail and when I spoke to her, she told me they were on their way to the hospital and the priest was reading my brother Brandon his last rites. She explained that she didn't want to see her son die and that Brandon was in a medicinal coma. It was horrible to hear my mother in that condition. But approximately a week after the doctor's last-ditch effort to save Brandon's life by putting a tube in his abdomen to drain the fluid out of it, my brother woke up and checked himself out of the hospital against the advice of his doctors. Sadly, that same day my brother went right back to injecting heroin. Miraculously, 24 months later he is still alive. I got to give it to him! He is a tough guy for sure.

Approximately two weeks after I lost my mother. I learned that my Aunt Linda, my mother's sister, had died of a massive heart attack, just like my mother. It was horrific. I called home to speak to my father and he dropped another bombshell on me! My younger brother Kenneth was now addicted to drugs and homeless. I suddenly realized this was all a strategic attack by the kingdom of darkness. The Bible says, "We wrestle not against flesh and blood, but against powers and principalities, and forces of darkness, and spiritual wickedness in high places" (Ephesians 6:12). There was no doubt Satan was attacking my family because he always fights the hardest when you're closest to your miracle.

I had already had a miracle. But now I was swimming in a sea of miracles, one right after another. I kept believing what God said about me and my situation, not what my circumstances said. I kept walking by faith and not by sight. I fixed my eyes on Jesus, the author and perfecter of my faith. I stayed grounded in the word of God. About six months later, after visiting with my sister Tammie, she told me my mother didn't kill herself. She had a massive heart attack. I was so relieved I cried for twenty minutes in the laundry room because I thought my mother had killed herself. I was grateful she didn't kill herself. But, it was still very difficult.

Then there would still be another family tragedy to deal with. I received a letter from the Department of Family Services back in Texas. The United States Marshalls had just gone and kicked in doors in two states to get my thirteen-year-old daughter back from being sex trafficked. I was destroyed emotionally. But I kept walking by faith and not by sight. I kept saying to myself, "I'm blessed and not cursed. My enemies will come at me from one way, but God will allow me to watch them flee from me in seven ways. God is fighting my battles for me."

Let me just say something. In my former life, there wouldn't have been a place on Earth where those people could hide that did that to my daughter. I would have hunted those people down like animals that did that to my daughter and sought retribution. But God taught me to love the sinner and hate the sin. I got down on my knees one day and said, "Lord God save me from being angry. If I get angry, God forbid me from sinning against you or my fellow man. I ask you God, "To forgive the people that did that to my daughter and let them find your love in Jesus Christ." I paused; my mind was racing. There was a battle of good and evil raging within me! I said, "God, I forgive my daughters' perpetrators for their sin against you and my child." That was one of the hardest things that I had ever done.

My prayer tested me to see if I would love the unlovable. But I know the secret and that is love carries no record of wrongs. It always forgives and I forgave them because I didn't want to harbor unforgiveness in my heart. That creates a very dangerous spiritual condition. Another thing was that God forgave me for all I had done in my former life. Also, there was this startling truth. That God is worthy of my obedience and I believe unforgiveness is a sin unto death.

After my family and I had been brutally assaulted by the kingdom of darkness that I had served so faithfully in my former life. I made a solemn vow to God to only fight the good fight of faith. I continued to work out my salvation with fear and trembling, according to the scriptures, one day at a time. I knew and believed that Almighty God, by way of his Holy Spirit, was in me acting according to his will and good pleasure.

I did my best by staying close to the Lord in my thoughts, emotions, attitudes, and actions. I kept on keeping on. In other words, I kept my eyes fixed upon Jesus. I kept helping others get sober, preaching, and teaching true freedom comes by the perfect law of liberty, which is the royal law of love. I kept loving God and my fellow man in truth and action.

The scriptures say, "Love the Lord your God with all your heart, body, mind, strength, and soul." It also says, "Love your neighbor as yourself, and treat others how you want to be treated." Most importantly the scriptures say, "No greater love can a man have than to lay down his life for his friend."

When I was lying in that holding cell that fateful day, I was withdrawing from heroin and decided to follow Jesus. I realized that day in, and day out, I needed to keep laying down my life for Jesus Christ, loving him like he first loved me. I needed to do this one day at a time.

Jesus laid down his life for humanity thousands of years ago. He did this so that we all could have a perfect example to live our lives. The word love is really spelled g-i-v-e. Jesus had given his life for me and bore my sins on the cross. Jesus did this to give you and I true life, abundant life, joy, peace, and contentment. Another thing I realized was why Jesus did this and it was so that we could all have an opportunity to take our rightful place in God's kingdom.

## THE DIFFERENCE MAKER

The good thing about knowing this was it gave me the ability to wake up one day at a time and continually surrender my life to God through Jesus Christ. That is exactly what I kept on doing.

It also helped me fully grasp that salvation is a supernatural work of God and is by faith and faith alone in Jesus Christ. The main thing that the Bible taught me about Jesus Christs' entire life was that the best sermon that I could ever preach was by the way I lived my life. Whatever I said, thought, or did. I did it out of faith in the name of the Lord Jesus Christ to the Glory of God. I put this principle into practice one moment at a time. That would turn out to be the difference maker in my thinking and we all know that thoughts, proceed our actions. I realized I needed to do it all for Jesus, to God's glory. I lived in this fundamental truth every day. That no matter what I was doing, I was doing it for Jesus. I was literally cleaning toilets for Jesus!

At that time there was a lot was going on in my life. Some good things and some bad things. There were times in my life when I was walking it out and if I hadn't been walking by faith, I would have given up a long time ago. There were times when Satan would inject a thought into my mind like you're never going to change, it's too hard, or you should give up. Another thought that went through my mind constantly was, your life is over and you are ruined forever. The good thing was that before I ever got to the situation that I was in, rather it was good or bad for me, I chose to stay in faith. I believed what my brother in Christ the Apostle Paul had written thousands of years before me. The Bible says, "All things work together for good to those who love the Lord and are called according to his purpose" (Romans 8:28).

I knew and believed that I was called according to God's purpose for my life. I lived and stood for the truth for the first time in my life. I also believed that no matter how many stumbling blocks the "Great Deceiver" Satan himself threw at me. I was going to stay in faith. I was going to walk by faith and not by sight and because I was walking by faith and not after the flesh, but after the spirit. I would be able to use what was meant by Satan to destroy me as a stepping stone to fulfill my God-given destiny. God makes that possible through his amazing saving and sustaining grace. I believe beyond a shadow of a doubt, that on those terms, I could do all things through Christ who strengthens me.

The good thing is that now I know and possess a knowledge of the scriptures that liberates me from the bondage of sin and self. The Bible says, "The righteous will live by faith." *"I believe what Dr. R.C. Sproul said, "The righteous live by trust. In other words, the thing that characterizes the righteous person above all else is an abiding trust in God and his promises. The righteous people trust the Lord, and because of this, they continue to believe in Him when He is slow to act. They don't just believe in God—they believe God" (Ligonier devotionals, 2014)."* Remember this as long as you live, faith equals belief. My point is that I had died to self that fateful day in that cell and chose a better life through faith in the Lord Jesus Christ. I surrendered my God-given free will and every detail of my life to God in Christ Jesus my Lord. Therefore I was dead to self. I had crucified my flesh in that manner. Then God's Holy Spirit could be exalted in my body to do his will and finish his work.

I realize now that I was put here on this earth to glorify God with my life. When we surrender our life to Christ, it is then and only then that God's Holy Spirit can be exalted in our bodies. That is the way God works in us, acting according to his will and good pleasure. The great thing about knowing this was that I realized I had the same power at work in me as Jesus Christ had working in him thousands of years before me. That good old resurrection power that raised Jesus Christ the son of God, from the grave. So technically, I was living a resurrected life and as long as I kept dying to self, one moment and one day at a time.

God in all his love, grace, and mercy, would continue to reach out to me and raise me back up from the depths of the grave one day at a time as I died to myself.

My problem in my former life was that I was very selfish. But I just kept on surrendering my life to the Lord daily and one miracle after another kept coming. But the great thing about all this at the time was that I didn't feel alone anymore. The reason why is that I had a relationship with God for the first time in my life. The good Lord had promised never to leave or forsake me and I truly believed that. Then it was like Jesus was telling the people around me to take off my grave clothes, just like he did Lazarus in the Bible. In other words, my old sinful self. I noticed the change that was occuring in my life and I was so thankful that Jesus kept working with me. The good Lord kept doing this through the people around me and the Bible.

I didn't first notice it. But when I was in the torture chamber (holding cell) going through heroin withdrawals. I came to know utter hopelessness and despair like few human beings ever experience. I was buried in complete hopelesness and despair. There were a million negative thoughts that overpowered me at that time. I was bombarded in my mind by this very negative, demonic thought process.

Looking back now, it is kind of crazy because I distinctly remember a thought in my head telling me, "It's over. You are finished. You've seen your best days. Your future is tainted. Your life is ruined." Yet there is a difference between being buried and being planted. That difference boils down to your expectation of what happens next.

*When you put a seed in the ground, you don't say, "I'm burying this seed." You say, "I'm planting this seed." The difference is when you plant a seed, you expect to see it rise again and come back to life. Now, there is a time and a place for burying and planting. For instance, I had a dog that died. I didn't say, "I'm planting this dog." I knew it wasn't coming back.*

*The time for planting comes when challenges arise. We all face difficulties, but you have the seed of Almighty God on the inside of you. He breathed his life into you. When you go through disappointments, and you're in tough times, You and I may feel like we have been buried, but the fact is, you've simply been planted. You go in as a seed, but because of the life of God, you come out blossomed, producing even more fruit. You come out twice as good as before.*

*Jesus talked about this in (John 12:24) when he said, "That unless a grain of wheat falls to the ground and is planted, it will not produce fruit." You can store a seed on a shelf for a lifetime. It will never become what it was created to be until you put it in the ground. Its potential will never be fully realized until it's planted. As long as it's up on a shelf where it is comfortable, its potential lies dormant.*

*The same holds true for people facing hard times. You can stay on the shelf. You don't have to stretch. You don't have to deal with adversity. In the meantime, your potential will remain locked up on the inside, dormant. Only after your seed has been planted and it goes through the process of germination—the outer shell breaks off, the new growth springs forth—will it blossom and produce more fruit. As time goes by, instead of being a little seed buried in the ground, it grows into a beautiful plant producing bright, colorful flowers.*

*What happened? The seed was planted. Like me, that seed had to go through dark times and lonely nights. That seed had to push tons of dirt out of the way. Sometimes, the seed, like me, felt like it would never see bright days, but like me, the seed pressed forward. Eventually, as God intended, like me, His creation burst through the darkness into the light, grew, and flourished.*

*I want to tell you something, my dear friend. No matter what comes against you in life, you pitch your tent in the land of hope through Christ Jesus. You are not buried. You are planted. You may feel as though you are buried in the dirt right now. You're in a tough time. Something was unfair. It seems like your situation will never change. But if you keep shaking off the dirt, shaking off the self-pity, shaking off the negative thoughts, then you too—like that little seed—will begin to feel the life of God spring forth. That same power that raised Christ from the dead is on the inside of you.*

## THE FARMER AND THE MULE

*I once heard a story about a farmer who had a mule that fell into an abandoned well sixty feet deep. The farmer was very fond of this old mule. The well was very narrow, and the mule was at the very bottom. The farmer knew there was no way to rescue the mule. The mule had not moved or made a single sound. The farmer figured the mule died in the fall.*

*He decided to leave the mule at the bottom of the abandoned well and fill it with dirt. The farmer called his sons to help shovel dirt down the well. The farmer was devastated. The first shovel load of dirt woke the mule who had been knocked out from the fall. When the mule felt the next load of dirt hit his back, he realized what was happening. But instead of letting himself be buried, the mule shook it off. Whenever a load of dirt hit his back, the mule shook his body, tossing the dirt to his hooves. Then he'd step out of it.*

181

*The mule kept it up. Shake and step. Shake and step. After nearly an hour of shoveling dirt, the farmer and his helpers were shocked to see the mule's ears appear at the top of the well. They realized that the mule was not dead. So they kept shoveling until the old mule stepped out of the well and walked to freedom. They'd come to bury the mule, but they raised him instead!*

The enemy of my soul came to bury me in Hancock County, but like that old mule, the good Lord raised me instead. *My friend, when you feel dirt hit your back, when life treats you unfairly, when you go through disappointments—don't let it bury you. Shake it off and step up with that resurrection power and a victor's mentality that says I can, and yes, I will be willing to go to any length to fulfill my God-given destiny at all costs because God is worthy.*

*As the wise mule figured out, the same dirt meant to bury you could also be your salvation. For you, it contains the seeds of your rebirth sent by Almighty God to promote you. Your attitude should be I'm down but not out, and this too shall pass. This difficulty was meant for my harm, but I know and believe what God says about my situation, and I know all things work together for good for those who love the Lord and are called according to his purpose.*

*You have to break out of that worldly mold and say to yourself, "I'm blessed and not cursed. I'm above and not beneath. I'm the head and not the tail. My enemies will come from me in one way. But I will watch them flee from me in seven ways. I will lend and not borrow. More importantly, you've got to know and believe what the Bible says about your situation"* (Osteen, 2009).

The same Almighty God that parted the Red Sea also healed the blind, healed the sick and sent his son Jesus, Jesus, Jesus, sweet precious Jesus, to save the lost and bring love and hope to a dying world. He sent his son to die for you and give you the victory over the enemy of your soul, Satan. You have to know the hope and victory that comes by way of God through Jesus Christ, his one and only son. Jesus laid down his life for you.

You have a friend that sticks closer than a brother in Jesus Christ, the son of the living God. Why don't you come out of the house of pain? To the house of God, knowing that God is unconditional love. You're searching for the love of God in Christ Jesus. I promise you nothing will fill that God-shaped void in your heart. I searched the world over and tried to stuff every false comforter that the world had to offer in that God-shaped void in my heart. I promise you this one thing. There is nothing that will fit but the love of God in Christ Jesus. The good Lord reserves the right to fill that void in your heart.

I beg of you not to waste one more minute of your life. Whether you're living in a penthouse, the penitentiary, or your own private prison that you built around your heart because you have been hurt. I don't care who you are. You need Jesus Christ as your savior to take your rightful place in eternity and creation. I'm asking you to allow the one and only true God to take his rightful place in your heart and life.

The greatest invitation I ever received was the invitation to follow Jesus. I have never been sorry. Every life is a story and every story matters. God wrote every page of your life. Your God-given destiny is greatness and I beg of you not to settle for a life of mediocrity.

Remember this no matter what happens to you in this lifetime. When you come to the end of your life. I promise you that there isn't but one thing going to matter and that is relationships. Meaning your relationship with God and his creation. Namely, people like you, who are God's prized possession, will matter the most.

I wasted forty-one years of my life on selfishness and self-centeredness. Please don't waste yours. I beg of you to die to self through Jesus Christ and let him be exalted in your body through the power of the Holy Spirit. You need to do this so that you can counter your natural state in the creation. We are all selfishness and self-centered. We can counter this state with a life of self-giving, by giving ourselves first to God and then to others. That is the true life and the abundant life that Jesus Christ talked about. The life that is crowned with a sense of purpose, joy, peace, and contentment.

I'm so grateful that God spared my life and gave me true life. But this book is not about me! Any more than this life about me. This book is about a terribly broken human being whom the loving, gracious God of Abraham, Isaac, and Jacob reached out and touched through Jesus Christ and transformed into the likeness of his son. In other words, it is about what God did through me. What God is trying to do through me now is to inspire you to follow Jesus.

More importantly, can you feel God knocking at the door of your heart? In the Bible Jesus said, "Behold! I stand at the door and knock. If anyone will answer, I will come in" (Revelation 3:20). My question to you today is "Will you answer the door and choose to have a relationship with God through Jesus Christ?"

Although it seemed like my life was becoming more and more difficult at times, I continued to work out my salvation with fear and trembling. I keep repeating this verse because it is important that you understand that we must do our part as Christians. Our part is to examine and test ourselves daily to be sure we are in the faith.

I kept busy as an inmate worker way back then. Even now to this very day, I consider it a true honor to be able to help my friends at the jail. I have never stopped helping the men and women of the Hancock County Sheriff's Office. I still work approximately fifteen hours a day, seven days a week. I also still teach two classes every week and a rehab every other month. I'm so grateful to God for being able to bless others and glorify God with my life. As I'm working, I often watch the officers very closely. I watch how they respond to the inmates in certain situations. The officers always treat the inmates and the public the way they want to be treated, within the boundaries and parameters of the rules of the Hancock County Jail and law.

I have learned some very valuable lessons from the good Lord through the officers here at the Jail. I'm eternally grateful to all of them for their service to Hancock County and for treating me with the utmost respect and dignity. God taught me a very valuable lesson through Captain Andrew Johnson. A lesson about enduring, persevering, and overcoming the challenges of life. Captain Andrew Johnson used to be in the air-conditioning business. But fourteen years ago, he got out of the business. Captain Johnson quit the business because it didn't have health insurance or a retirement plan. He was married and needed a future for his family. He decided to take a pay cut and come to work at the Hancock County Sheriff's Office as a correctional officer.

Captain Johnson started at the bottom of the totem pole, so to speak. He started as a correctional officer working the floor. Then he got promoted to Sergeant. He then quickly worked his way up through the ranks all the way to Lieutenant. In 2014 he was passed over for the Assistant Warden position. But Lieutenant Johnson then decided to keep doing his very best and then the opportunity came again for him to be the Assistant Warden in 2021. He got the promotion that time without any question or hesitation.

Captain Andrew Johnson could have easily been bitter, resentful, or angry. But he didn't get out of character. He just kept being his very best. He knew he wasn't buried; he was planted! He knew his time was coming. He knew what I know today. He was waiting for the next opportunity. He knows what I'm telling you. That no, just simply means you need to seek your next opportunity. Sometimes, no means God is preparing you to get the promotion, increase, or favor. But you are not ready to receive it yet. Again, Johnson did what I told you earlier; he kept walking by faith and not by sight. I like the way Joel Osteen said, *"He shook off the dirt, so to speak, like that old mule stuck in the bottom of the well and stepped right into his God-given destiny"* (Osteen, 2009). I was honored enough to help him clean his new office and help him move into it the day he took the position. One of his most famous one-liners is, "It's not personal; it is just business." I must say that Captain Johnson is one of the fairest men in the business.

Then there was a Correctional Officer D. Foster who taught me a valuable life lesson. What he taught me was that if you love someone, you have to let them go. If they come back to you, it was meant to be. If they don't, it wasn't meant to be. I became very close with Correctional Officer D. Foster and learned a lot from him. Sadly, one day he got a different job and then quit. I was devastated because I had worked with him for years. Make no mistake, I'm not saying that the officers look at me as their friend. I look at them as my friends. The officers have a job to do and I observe them maintain custody, care, and control of the inmates at the Hancock County Jail daily. They are all very professional, and in all of my years of being incarcerated, I have never witnessed a more professional group of people with as much compassion as them. Anywhere I have been locked up in America!

All the Hancock County Sheriff's Office officers have treated me with the utmost dignity and respect. I really appreciate all the lessons I have been taught through them over the years. Especially my boss Jimbo. He taught me that being kind to someone doesn't cost anything. He shows up to work every day at seventy-nine years old with a good attitude and has treated me better than I deserved. I hope God blesses him in everything he does. Jimbo is a great example of what a human being should be like. I'm truly grateful to be able to work for him. There is nobody that I'm closer to than Jimbo.

I want to thank the medical staff for allowing me to work for them all these years and for being the kindest, sweetest souls in the business, and helping me with my medical conditions all throughout my stay here. I hope God blesses them in everything they do. Amazingly the men and women at the Hancock County Sheriff's Office all believed in what was left of that bright young kid from Arlington, Texas. They put blind faith in me when they didn't have to. They believed in me to do my job when they didn't know anything about me and even when I stopped believing in myself. When I thought my life was over and nobody cared. I still can't believe it to this day. The good lord would use the Hancock County Sheriff's Office to inspire me to change my life. Wow!

# THE CODE OF SILENCE—OMERTA

The irony of this whole thing is that I was taught never to cooperate with the police under any circumstance in my former life. When the loving, gracious God that I serve today reached out to me through the Hancock County Sheriff's Office and loved me back to my rightful place in creation. My point is that in my darkest hour, when it looked as if I was buried, it was as if God spoke and said, "Not this one, Satan. This one is planted and not buried; you can't have him." God's way of doing this was unique and not in a way I could have ever imagined. The good Lord decided to do this through the people I was told never to trust. Through the Hancock County Sheriff's Office. I hear a lot of bad stuff about the Police. I'm sure some cops make bad decisions, just like we all have, but I know beyond a shadow of a doubt that there are many more good cops than bad. I see the Hancock County Sheriff Deputies risk their lives daily to protect their community. I really believe personally after all these years. The cops don't get enough credit for what they do; they have a very difficult job and are underpaid. After all the years I have spent on this roller coaster ride called life. I finally feel like I made it home. To my Heavenly home and my Earthly home, Hancock County.

I come to this conclusion and firmly believe that it is only fitting to come back to Hancock County and open up a rehab when I get out of prison. After thirty years of being held captive by the enemy of my soul. I have finally received God's grace. I want to tell you something that you should never forget. God never one time forsook me. He was there fighting for me every step of the way. I just couldn't see it because these things are spiritually discerned.

About a year and a half ago, I was sitting in the laundry of the jail. I was praying to the Lord about my third wife Nicki. At first, I was asking God to restore my relationship with her. I had prayed for my third wife off and on for months. Finally, after deafening silence from the throne room of heaven, I was in deep sorrow. I knew one of two things was happening. I already knew the answer and God was testing me to act out of faith or I was praying out of selfish motives. I knew I was scripturally free from that marriage because of adultery by both parties. I was willing to forgive her no matter what to save my marriage and glorify God with my life. But then I heard a small voice in my spirit say, "Move on, son." I then prayed for her and said, "God, please let Nicki find someone to love her like I should have, but more importantly, let her find your love in Christ Jesus." It was over and I was done with her finally and forever.

I had been through a lot and I had caused myself a lot of problems. More importantly, I had caused other people who really loved me many problems-Nicki. Even though I was out of the darkness and into the light. It didn't take me long to figure out that I was still trying to salvage the past. It was almost as if it was bittersweet. But God would not have any part of that. I just knew and believed God would make my life right in the end. God spoke to me and said, "Forget those things which are behind and press toward the mark, for the high calling of Me son in Christ Jesus." I believe wholeheartedly that God is opening doors for me that no man can shut. The gist of my telling you this is that I filed for divorce after going through everything I just told you with Nicki and approximately one week after I filed the paperwork. She died in her sleep. The last time I ever talked to her, she hung up on me. The really sad part is that I found all this out five months after she died. I was deeply saddened.

But I kept walking by faith and trusting in the Lord. I really believe that if we could see what Almighty God is doing behind the scenes for our life, that it would take our breath away. God's timing is impeccable. At just the right time, I know God will bring all of my dreams to pass. My friend, no matter who you are, never forget your identity in Christ. You are a child of the most high God. You got royal blood flowing through your veins. I believe and declare that you will come to the fullness of your God-given destiny.

Don't believe the lies of the enemy, believe what the Bible says about you, and speak positive faith-filled words over your life and the lives of others. Let go and let God bring love and hope to a dying world through you. God is worthy of the glory, honor, and praise in your life! There is no doubt in my mind that He is worthy. I'm not concerned with my eternal destiny anymore. It is written in stone. In the "The Lambs Book of Life." I'm concerned with your eternal destiny. I'm concerned with your relationship with God through his son Jesus Christ. I'm concerned with whether or not you know your eternal value.

I'm begging you to answer the door of your heart. Can you hear it? That is Jesus knocking at the door. Will you please receive him today and let him take his rightful place in your heart and life? I hope you find what you're searching for before you step from this life, through the doorway of death, into eternity. I beg of you not to waste your life. You only get one life. Don't be like me and put all the false comforters the world has to offer in the place where Almighty God should be in your heart and life. I implore you to receive the love of God in Christ

Jesus. You need Jesus so that you can fill that God-shaped void in your heart and have peace with God and your fellow man. Don't waste thirty years of your life like me.

There was a whole lot of me in my former life and that selfishness almost led me to my death. Maybe you feel like you have already wasted too many years. I assure you that everything is going to be ok. You can't make a brand-new start. But you can make a brand-new ending. Remember that the wages of sin is death, but the free gift of God is eternal life through Jesus Christ. Today is your day to make a brand-new ending! You have a friend in Jesus Christ. Please accept the invitation to follow Jesus. There is an old gospel song that I used to listen to when I was about eight years old and sing with my mother. The main chorus line was I have decided to follow Jesus, I have decided to follow Jesus, no turning back, no turning back. I hope and pray that you have decided to follow Jesus because that is what you're searching for, no matter who you are. It doesn't matter who you are or where you live. If you live in a penthouse, the penitentiary, or you're an addict that has lost it all and only lives to use, abuse drugs, and sleep on a park bench, you need Jesus Christ. Almighty God wants a relationship with you no matter who you are or what you have done because you're his creation!

The grace of God is unfathomable. I want to speak to you about how God used the Sheriff's Office to affirm that I had received his grace. On February 1, 2021 a Lieutenant on patrol responded to a call on the NorthSide of Hancock County. I knew this particular officer very well. I had spoken with him on his way out the door that morning. I said, "You be safe out there, Lieu!" I say that just about every morning to the patrol officers as they are leaving the briefing room. I often washed this

Lieutenant's patrol vehicle. He was killed in the line of duty later on that day.

## AFFIRMATION THAT I HAD RECEIVED GOD'S GRACE

I was one of two inmates that got the blessing to go to work at the funeral and help set up, clean up, and serve food. The other inmate and I were both from Texas. We helped the county prepare for the funeral service. There was such an outpouring of heartfelt unity from all over the state of Mississippi and the United States. I remember it like it was yesterday. It was a beautiful day in February. The sun was shining bright in the sky. There were streets blocked off and cars were parked everywhere on the city streets. People were lined up and down Interstate 10 all the way to Biloxi, Mississippi. I heard the funeral procession was fifteen miles long. Fire trucks were on the overpasses with American flags hanging from their ladders, perched high in the air.

The other inmate and I stayed in the kitchen during the funeral service. Then shortly after the funeral. The Lieutenant's fellow officers of which were the pallbearers, started carrying the casket out of the building. The pallbearers stopped right where the family of the fallen officer was sitting. All the officers from the Lieutenant's shift were standing at attention right in front of the casket. I looked around and the media was everywhere. It was almost as if time had stopped.

Then the dispatcher came over all the radios and a speaker hooked up where everyone could hear it. The dispatcher said, "H-53." She repeated, "H-53." Then the third time, the dispatcher said, "H-53, please respond." Obviously, he would never respond again on this side of Heaven. The law enforcement community calls that "The last call." I want to tell you something. I could never describe to you in a million lifetimes how brutal that last call to H-53 was for everybody at the funeral. It was heart-wrenching, and as all of this was going on. I suddenly looked to my left and saw a black Firebird. I couldn't believe my eyes; that race car belonged to the Lieutenant. We talked about that car on several occasions. They were literally going to take his race car to the funeral. The Lieutenant loved that car. I had also heard others talk about how much he liked that car.

I could hear the bagpipes playing Amazing Grace and the hail of gunfire from a twenty-one-gun salute. There wasn't a dry eye around for miles. It was terrible. I then looked to my left; the bagpipes were still playing Amazing Grace. I saw a father down on one knee and he was attending to a little girl. I was in shock and I instantly thought about my life. I thought about my three daughters Alice, Brenda, and Elaina. I thought about the Lieutenant. How he was a great man, he served his country in the United States Air Force, and his community as a police officer. He always had a smileon his face and he always spoke kindly to everyone, including me. I thought about his wife and two kids. I also thought about how much I had changed and had been inspired to change my life by the brave men and women at the Hancock County Sheriff's Office, who risk their lives daily to protect and serve their community. I couldn't understand why the Lieutenant was in that casket. A great human being and here I was, a reformed liar, cheat, thief, con, swindler, and master manipulator in my former life, and the good Lord let me live.

I thought about how the Lieutenant would never be able to call home and tell his family he loved them again, how he had made the ultimate sacrifice. Then it came to me. The Lieutenant had literally laid down his life for his friends, his fellow man, so they could live, just like Jesus did. I realized the Lieutenant's death and the song that was blaring on those bagpipes really said it all! Amazing Grace, how sweet the sound that saved a wretch like me, I once was lost, but now I'm found. I was blind, but thank you Lord God, now I see.

I suddenly realized that I had been fighting everyone and everything for so long. I didn't know how to surrender my life to the Lord. I didn't know how to stop fighting everyone and everything and trust the good Lord, even though I was learning more and more how to surrender my life to the Lord one day at a time. At that moment, Almighty God was reaching out to me and saying, "Son, you're going to be okay because you have received my grace." I was shaken to the core of my being and it was shocking to me. I am sharing this to tell you that God's grace is more promiscuous than I was in my former life with women.

It is God's will that no one should perish and all should come to the knowledge of Christ. God loves you and has a plan for your life no matter what you have done. You have a friend in Jesus Christ. Through the Lieutenant's death and continuing to work out my salvation with fear and trembling. I realized that God would not allow a trial to come into my life unless He had a purpose for it. When my mother went to be with the Lord in 2020. I walked out of the booking the very next day. I looked up and Sheriff Ricky Adam was right there. He said, "Mr. O'Dell, I heard you got some bad news about your mother last night. I want you to know that I'm very sorry to hear your mom passed away." I dropped my head, looked back up at him, and said, "I did, sir, but I know God is still on the throne." It was very difficult. But I knew that at the time, although it seemed as if I was buried, the god of this world, which is Satan and his kingdom of darkness, was wreaking havoc on my soul from every angle. I wasn't buried, I was planted, and I was coming back!

I kept telling myself, "I know God is going to make my righteousness shine like the dawn and the justice for my cause like the noonday sun" (Psalm 37:6). I knew that although my circumstances and situations said, "It was over and I was finished," that sometimes God asks us to believe things that contradict what we see with our eyes. I knew if I wanted to see his promises come to pass. I would have to learn to listen with my spiritual ears. I just kept walking by faith and not by sight.

I remembered the positive, faith-filled words that Dan and Joan Munger, Pat Burke, Tony, Jay and Rhonda Gamble, Warden Brandon Zeringue, Captain Johnson, and so many others kept speaking over me. I knew that although I felt all alone at times. Especially at the time of my mother's death. I wasn't alone; if God is for me, what can stand against me? But in the book of John 16:31, when Jesus spoke to the disciples about sending the Holy Spirit, he said, "A time is coming when you will be scattered, each to his own home. In fact, that time is already here. You will leave me and I will be alone. But I am never really alone because my Father is with me." STOP! READ THAT LAST LINE AGAIN, PLEASE! You and I are never alone, my friend. God is for you and with you!

I often felt like all the odds on earth were stacked against me. The enemy kept telling me it was over. You're finished; you have wrecked your life and you're not going to change. But I just kept being deaf to the negative. I turned the radio station in my head back to that channel from the most powerful transmitter in the universe, whose disc jockey was Almighty God himself. The good Lord is the greatest odd's maker in the universe. It was kind of crazy because for the first time in my life. I not only believed what the word of God said about me and my life. But I was living it and I was walking it out.

I knew God was in control of my destiny. I kept saying to myself, "God and I are a majority! God you are my vindicator. God, you are preparing a table for me in the presence of my enemies." I also knew and believed Satan is the real enemy, not people. I kept saying to myself, "This didn't come to stay. It came to pass. If God is for me, what can stand against me? The battle belongs to the Lord. Jesus already gave me the victory. I'm staying in faith and believing what Almighty God says about my situation. I'm blessed and not cursed despite my circumstances. I will rise again. I'm planted. I'm not buried."

On the day of my mother's death. I stepped out back to get some fresh air. Then Satan injected a thought into my mind. He said, "You robbed your mother of sixteen years of your life by being locked up." I spoke out loud on purpose and said, "You're right Satan and all those years I served you ignorantly, may the Lord rebuke you! But I know my mother forgives me of that, God has forgiven me, and I have forgiven myself." At that very moment, I realized that I had a clear conscience before God. I completely neutralized the enemy of my soul, Satan, the "Great Deceiver" himself, through my faith in the Lord Jesus Christ. I would never for one more moment of my life, live a lie. I bowed my head and thanked God that my past was in the past and that He had forgiven me. Therefore who am I not to forgive myself?

The point to all of this is that you and I have to be deaf to the negative. We have to believe what Almighty God says about us, not this world, or the enemy of our souls, Satan. You and I as Christians have that resurrection comeback power working in us. We have the light of life in us and his name is Jesus Christ. You must understand this Bible verse, "To live is Christ, and to die is gain" (Philippians 1:21). You might ask, what does this mentality have to do with transformation? It has everything to do with it. In our natural state of mind, we are selfish and self-centered. Our mind naturally steers us toward our desires instead of Almighty God's. Our life is all about us and we are defeated by our sin problem. But through the renewing of our mind with the Bible and the Lord Jesus Christ, we can walk in the victory God gave us through Jesus Christ. We are like a seed on a shelf when we don't have a relationship with our Creator. We will never realize our full potential without bowing to the one and only true God of Abraham, Isaac, and Jacob. He has all power and his name is Jehovah. He is not the God of our understanding. He is who He is and will become what he chooses to become, to fulfill his purpose.

Religion, Babylon the Great! Well, let's just say it will help you be a better person. But sadly the best you can be without Jesus Christ as your savior is terrible in God's eyes. According to God's righteous standard. In the Bible, Jesus says, "Greater love hath no man than this, that one lay lay down his life for his friends" (John 15:13, KJV). The great thing for us is that Jesus Christ died for us on the cross. He took the punishment for our sins. He set the example so that we all should live by in life. The Bible says, "The wages of sin is death, but the free gift of God is eternal life in Christ Jesus" (Romans 6:23, ERV). Jesus took our death, for our sins, so that we could receive the gift of God, which is eternal life through Christ Jesus. Jesus died so that we could all have true life. Then he was raised again on the third day and defeated death, so that we could be resurrected from a spiritual death, find true life, glorify God with our lives and help others break free from the kingdom of darkness.

I want to ask you two questions. Will you lay down your life like Jesus Christ did to glorify God and in view of God's mercy, offer your body as a living sacrifice? The second question is will you deny yourself, taking up your cross and following him daily? If you love God in truth and in action you will! But if you're giving God lip service you will not. When you lay down your life for the Lord. Then you will automatically lay down your life for your fellow man. All of this will come automatically because you will understand that they are God's creation and this will all be to God's glory. The motive of your heart will be that God is worthy. When you understand this principle that is called surrender. This will enable to automatically be obedient to the two greatest commandments in the Bible. The greatest commandment in the Bible is, "And you shall love the Lord your God with all your heart, body, mind, soul, and strength" (Mark 12:30). The second greatest commandment in the Bible is, "You shall love thy neighbor as yourself and treat others like you want to be treated" (Mark 12:31). My case and point is that transformation comes by way of renewing your mind through God's word. But it also comes through the living word, Jesus Christ, and the power of God's Holy Spirit of truth. Remember, the truth will set you free. But this principle is not just about you telling the truth. The Bible says, "Those who the son sets free, are free indeed" (John 8:36). To have true freedom and transformation, it must come, by the way, the truth, and the life—Jesus Christ, through the Bible, truth, by way of God's Holy Spirit of Truth, the same spirit that resurrected Jesus Christ from the dead. These three truths bring true freedom to the human race by way of the heart and mind, where most people like me are stuck in a prison of pride and selfishness.

# GOD WILL NEVER FORSAKE YOU

I heard a great man of faith named Dan Munger say, "There are no coincidences in the kingdom of God." Today I know and believe that statement wholeheartedly. As I look back on my life, I know and believe the good Lord has been right there with me every step of the way. God has never forsaken me, not even for a single second. At times in my life I have to admit that it seemed like God was a million miles away. But knowing what I know now. I realize that I felt like that because of my ignorance of the Bible, unwillingness to do my part, and unwillingness to surrender my life to the Lord. It was all because of my selfishness and self-centeredness, which is pride at its best. Pride is the exaltation of oneself. I know pride is the source of all sin and selfishness is the epitome of sin. That was the root of all my troubles.

When I truly trusted God unconditionally with my life. Then and only then did I find the peace of God, which surpasses all understanding like the Apostle Paul talked about. When I died to myself and stepped outside myself, my world instantly got bigger. This didn't occur until I chose to help others trapped like I was with their sin problem. I wouldn't trade my life today inside the walls of the Hancock County Jail with Jesus Christ as my commanding officer, to live a thousand years in my former life on my best day.

I was a successful failure. In other words, I failed in my personal life, but was very successful in business. I know now that true riches come from God. You can't buy them. I realize now that the greatest gift you can ever receive is free. It is the grace of the loving, gracious God we serve. He is worthy and I thank God every day for sending his son to die for me on the cross. The greatest thing about Christ dying for us while we were sinners, is the fact that if I die to myself one day at a time, it is then that God by way of his Holy Spirit, can be exalted in my body to do his will and finish his work. I then glorify God in my death to self and become Christ-like in this manner. When this happens, I'm a success in God's kingdom and more importantly it is all by God's righteous standard. In other words, I counter my former life of selfishness with a life of self-giving. I give my life to God first and then to others.

It is my sincere hope that when they read my eulogy. That the one main common denominator that the people would say about me at my funeral is that I loved the Lord with all my heart and I loved people unconditionally, just like Almighty God loves all of creation. Today I know and believe beyond a shadow of a doubt, that the one matters; every life is God's story and God wrote every page of this book of our lives. He is a personal God and every hair on our head is counted by the creator of the universe. We were predestined for greatness before forming in our mother's womb. We are a masterpiece in the Lord's eyes.

Looking back now and how far I have come from where I was. I realize that it is truly an honor to be used as a vessel of God's love in Christ Jesus. It is such a blessing to know that God wants to use us, to say by our actions, that He loves the world. The only question is that will you be willing to allow God to use you to do his will and finish his work? He can't do this without you surrendering your God-given free will and every detail of your life. The truth is that I have come to realize that life is a precious gift from God and it is not our life to squander. We are just good or bad stewards and our life belongs to God through Jesus Christ. Our salvation came at the cost of the life of God's only son. If you want true life and freedom, you must understand that you must lose your life to save it. After all these years of insanity. I finally learned that I could trust in the Lord. The question is, will you trust the Lord unconditionally? I hope you do, I hope you are and I hope you continue to all the days of your life. You got a true friend in Jesus!

As I write the last few pages of this book, I know I'm just a messenger. A good steward of God's time, talents, works, and possessions. I wish I could walk it out for you, but I'm just anointed to be James Odell. You have got to do your part. I realize I am nothing without Jesus for the first time in my life and coincidentally, I'm nothing with Christ either because I died to self. I can do nothing without a relationship with Jesus Christ, but I can do all things through Christ who strengthens me. But this only happens when I admit I'm powerless over my sin problem. The Apostle Paul said, "So I'm not the one living now— it is Christ living in me, I still live in my body, but I live by faith in the son of God. He is the one who loved and gave himself for me" (Galatians 2:20). My life is hidden with God in Christ Jesus my Lord. I also realize that I can and will do all things to the Glory of God. I also have come to know that nothing is impossible with God. The reason why is very simple, God and I are a majority.

In retrospect, as I look back on my life, I accomplished a lot, especially in business. But out of everything I have ever done in my lifetime. I realize now that the best choice that I have ever made was deciding to follow Jesus Christ. I want to state for the record that I lived in bondage because of the decisions I made and I take full responsibility for them. It seemed as if every decision that I had ever made in my life was bad. But look at me now, all because of one great decision to follow Jesus Christ. I'm transformed into a new creature. I'm not rehabilitated because being rehabilitated is about what I did. My transformation is about what God did for and through me. This came through his son Jesus Christ, on the cross. I always point to the cross. It was at the cross that the loving, living, gracious God we serve chose to heal all of humanity's brokenness. Did I play a part? Yes through my rigorous honesty, my open-mindedness to change and last but not least, I was willing to walk toward the Light of Life, Jesus Christ! Like that old gospel hymn goes, "I have decided to follow Jesus, I have decided to follow Jesus, no turning back, NO TURNING BACK!" I ask you to make the best decision you will ever make for your eternity and decide to follow Jesus. I know that some might say that I got lucky and defied the odds. I defied the odds, no doubt. But not because of me or anything I did; it was because "He who is in me, is greater than he who is in the world" ( 1 John 4:4)! Jesus Christ defeated the god of this world at the cross. Jesus also defeated sin, sickness, disease, and death. All for our spiritual freedom and to give us an option of where we will spend eternity. There is no doubt that I defied the odds. But only because God is the greatest odds maker in all of creation.

I thank God every day for sparing my life, giving me true and eternal life. It has been a priveiledge to serve the Lord and I'm truly grateful that God has allowed me to serve him. I pray each day that God will be first place in everything I say, think, and do. What is so amazing is that when I look back on my life. I can see the good Lord at work in my life, fighting for me valiantly, trying to get me to where I needed to be in eternity. Trying to get me to change my eternal destination and perception from a biblical perspective.

## THE WARDEN

In the early part of the millennium, right around the turn of the century, I was arrested at the Texas and Mexico border. I was coming back to the United States from Nuevo Laredo, Mexico. I was down there partying and up to no good. I was setting up a deal with some wise guys down there. I had been praying for deliverance from alcoholism and a broken heart. Coincidentally, a young man named Brandon Zeringue, who would later become the Warden of the Hancock County Jail, was just starting his career as a correctional officer in the Orleans Parish Prison. The good Lord knew exactly what He was doing. He was positioning the future Warden of the Hancock County Jail to receive me approximately seventeen years later. The reason for this was that without the good Lord putting favor in the Warden's heart for me, nothing would happen for me in Hancock County. I know this for a fact, beyond a shadow of a doubt.

Then, in 2005 Warden Brandon Zeringue was transferred to Mississippi from Louisiana. He would become a floor officer at the Harrison County Jail. I believe wholeheartedly that God knew I needed his favor and was helping him work his way up the ranks of the correctional industry. I believe God did this so that the Warden could be there to help people like Dan and Joan Munger to help me change my life. Coincidentally, it was right around this time that I was drowning in a sea of alcohol, cocaine, and women out in Las Vegas, Nevada, in 2005. I was begging the Lord to help me stop drinking and gambling. The crazy part was that although I was with women the whole time. I felt like I was the loneliest man on the planet. It was starting to set in that something was terribly wrong with me. I began to notice that it was almost as if an unseen force was working against me. I was lonely, oppressed, depressed, hurt, angry, and outright indignant at the world. I didn't realize it at the time, but the god of this world, Satan, had crowned me with mammon and made me the leader of my own demise.

At the time, I hated myself for walking out on Suzanne and my two daughters Alice and Brenda, six years earlier. The really sad part about all of this is that in the end, it would take me twenty-one years to forgive myself and heal from that mistake. That one mistake almost caused me to drink myself to death. I hated myself for hurting them. I lived in absolute agony because I abandoned them. I realize they needed me as much as I need them. I'm very sorry for that mistake. If I had consumed all of the tequila in Tijuana, Mexico, at the time, it wouldn't have comforted me. But God, who is so rich in mercy, was working on me at that point in my life. And although my willingness to change just wasn't there, God was working behind the scenes to get me to where I needed to be.

## THE CAPTAIN

At about the same time that Warden Zeringue was transferred to the Harrison County Jail in 2005. There was a correctional officer named Andrew Johnson that was beginning his career at the Hancock County Jail. In 2011, approximately six years later, Brandon Zeringue became the Captain of the Hancock County Jail under a different Sheriff. This is very significant because I would have to have Sheriff Ricky Adam win the election. So that Brandon Zeringue could get the promotion to Warden, and in turn, this would ensure that Lieutenant Andrew Johnson would go on and become the Captain. This is so important because I would need to have all these people's favor to change my life in Hancock county and be able to help others in the process. Approximately one year after Warden Zeringue made the rank of Captain, I was getting out of prison for the first time in 2012. While in prison, I had been reading the

Bible three to five times a day, praying for deliverance and healing from alcohol. Sadly, I just wasn't serious with God at the time and didn't understand the process of salvation and transformation. The great thing was God is so merciful and kept working on my heart and mind. Mainly through the Bible and I believe that God had a plan that was better than anything that I could have ever imagined.

## THE SHERIFF

It was in 2012 that a new Sheriff, named Ricky Adam was elected, the same year that I got out of prison for the first time. This is significant because my sin is becoming full-grown and I'm running out of time to change. But now Andrew Johnson has climbed his way all the way up the ladder (so to speak) and made the rank of Lieutenant at the Hancock County Jail. Remember that I need God to give me his favor through Sheriff Ricky Adam, Warden Brandon Zeringue, and Lieutenant Andrew Johnson. The new Sheriff getting elected is very significant. The reason why is very simple. I believe that if this didn't occur, I wouldn't have gotten the help I needed. The reason why is really simple, because Warden Brandon Zeringue and Captain Andrew Johnson at this time probably wouldn't be the Warden and the Captain at the jail now. If another Sheriff wins the election, he might promote one of his own to a high-ranking position, which is often the case.

Ricky Adam was the new Sheriff, former real estate agent, and judge. This would be a game changer for my life and law enforcement in Hancock County. It was a game changer because at this moment in time in 2012. The good Lord was getting all these men together at the same time and place to be high-ranking members at the Sheriff's Office. The great thing is that God would put a ton of favor in these men's hearts for me. Another thing was that Sheriff Ricky Adam saw something as a judge that most people never hear or know about. The Sheriff knew all too well that as a judge, your hands are often tied because you have to stay within the boundaries of the law. I heard Sheriff Ricky Adam say, "That he knew that the courts are reactive instead of proactive." So that is one major reason why Sheriff Ricky Adam got into law enforcement: by being proactive, you can help more people.

The great thing about this was that Sheriff Ricky Adam would not only employ people that were professionals, but amazingly he would hire officers who cared about people. In the end, I believe that Sheriff Ricky Adam's mentality to help others inspired me to change my life. And it would be God working through Sheriff Ricky Adam that would inspire him to put all the right people, in all the right places, to do heart surgery of a magnitude on me that is indescribable. All of this was done even though I was a stranger to Hancock County and nobody in the small town of Bay St. Louis, Mississippi, even knew who I was.

You have to understand something. I'm a habitual criminal and I have been arrested twenty-four times in four states. Even though nobody knew me in this town from Adam and Eve when I was arrested that fateful night, these people at the Sheriff's Office put good faith in me as a habitual criminal and total stranger. That is hard to get people to do in any town, especially in small town America. Then after all that, the good Lord inspired me to change my life through them. That my friend is a miracle in itself!

I was taught never to trust the cops in my former life. Let me state for the record I never did trust the cops for one moment of my former life. The Bible says, "There is a way which seemeth

206

right unto a man, but the end thereof are the ways of death" (Proverbs 14:13 KJV). God did all this through these people and not while I was a good person. But when I was at my worst as a human being. Just like Jesus Christ died for us while we were sinners. The Bible says, "To love the sinner, and hate the sin." The people at the Hancock County Sheriff's Office could have easily said, "No thanks, we don't trust him." I wouldn't have blamed them if they had said that. But they gave me a chance to change my life and put blind faith in me. I'm so grateful to the people of Hancock County for helping me. I want to thank Sheriff Ricky Adam for allowing me to be a Sheriff's Worker for the past four years. It has been one of my greatest honors and a privilege.

There was one time I was speaking to Sheriff Adam about my life. I said, "In my former life I was a terrible human being." The Sheriff looked straight at me and said, "There aren't any terrible human beings, only terrible decisions." I realized right then and there that I could never forget that statement. At that moment, I understood that the Sheriff was right and that we all have sinned and fallen short of the glory of God. I also realized that I needed to stop judging myself and others. Most importantly, I realized that I needed to love the sinner and hate the sin. I also realized that I should practice these principles with myself and others. My reason for doing these things would be that I want to be a better example of the love of God in Christ Jesus. I then began to focus on bettering myself and others every day. The reason why the Sheriff's statement to me was so significant is really very simple. If you believe there are terrible human beings, you will just walk away from them and deny them the unconditional love of God in Christ Jesus, which abounds to you and through you, by the power of the Holy Spirit. Another reason is that God is Love and is in us acting according to his will and good pleasure. It is when we understand this principle that we can die to self one day at a time and let God be exalted in our bodies by his Holy Spirit. But only if you're a true follower of Christ.

I believe it helps to know God's will for all of his creation. It is God's will that no one should perish and that all of us should come to the knowledge of Christ. God loves people for who they are and where they're at, not by what they do, and He does this through us. This is why Jesus Christ, the son of God, died on the cross for us. He did this while we were dead in our sins to prove that unconditional love is real. Coincidentally, the Bible says, "God is Love" (1 John 4 8-16). In 2013, when I went to prison for the second time, I began to pray without ceasing for a miracle. I didn't know it at the time. But by this time, Warden Brandon Zeringue had climbed his way all the way to the top of the correctional industry and had become the Assistant Warden of the Hancock County Jail. When the Sheriff won the election and Brandon Zeringue became the Assistant Warden at the jail, that put me in the perfect position, for the good Lord to love me back to my rightful place in creation and resurrect me from the depths of the grave at the Hancock County Jail.

## COINCIDENCE—I THINK NOT

God knew I didn't have enough faith to change. But, the good Lord is so gracious and decided to use the people around me to love me through all of this until I could believe and love myself. Coincidentally, one year before Brandon Zeringue became the Captain at the Hancock County Jail. I was still begging for deliverance from alcoholism and a broken heart in 2013. I had already shipwrecked my life again. I wasn't out of prison for sixteen months when I decided to commit another felony. I wound up going back to prison in September 2013. I didn't recognize it at the time. But God was already at work and had a date set for me to step into my God-given destiny.

Remember when I told you that a preacher from Ft. Worth, Texas, said, "Son, you're poised for a miracle." In other words, I needed a miracle, and that preacher knew what I didn't in 2013. Only God could give me the miracle I so desperately needed, and it would be through the people around me. All my hurts came from people, and God would heal me through people, also. Why did I remember what the preacher said? I had spoken to thousands of people since then. Why was that seared into my mind? Some might say it is protein memory bumps on the brain called dendritic spines. (I love science!) I'm kidding. It is really simple for me, though. The truth is that what the preacher told me that day was of divine inspiration. I believe that was God's way of saying, "You did it your way and failed. Now I will show you my power is made perfect in weakness."

What I didn't know then, but I know now, is unless you lose all hope in self-righteousness, you are doomed and can't have a relationship with the Living Hope, which is Almighty God, through faith in the Lord Jesus Christ. The good thing for me was that the good Lord behind the scenes was already answering my prayers for deliverance. Commander Dan Munger (retired) was appointed to serve as the volunteer chaplain at the Hancock County Jail shortly before 2013. Coincidentally, this was under Sheriff Ricky Adam's administration. The crazy thing is that as I look back now. During this time I was essentially dying in my sin, so my life was in the worst shape it had ever been in. At the time things were getting worse, but I had one good thing going for me. The good Lord already had all the right people, in all the right places, at the Hancock County Jail. Although it seemed like my prayers were unanswered at the time, God had already started to answer them in a way that I could have never have imagined. God was working behind the scenes as I was lost in my sin to save me from destruction. I was praying for deliverance the whole time. I had been praying since I was at the border of Texas and Mexico, in jail awaiting extradition, the same year Brandon Zeringue started his career as a correctional officer in 2001. At the time it seemed like God was a million miles away. But now I know that the good Lord was right there with me the entire time. I just didn't have enough faith to see it.

Another major coincidence was on the fateful night I was arrested in Mississippi, coming out of Slidell, Louisiana. Right before I got to Mississippi, there was the Slidell, Louisiana cop, that was behind me for at least five minutes after I noticed him. Then he drove down the exit quickly and looked straight at me to identify me. I had just done a shot of heroin driving down the highway. Why did he decide to hand me off, so to speak, to the Hancock County Sheriff's Office, instead of arresting me and putting me in jail in Louisiana? That officer had the authority and probable cause to pull me over with the warrant in the National Crime Information Center. If any law enforcement officer had run a check of the tags on my truck, it would immediately come back positive for a warrant. I believe God prevented me from being arrested in Louisiana because if I had been arrested in Louisiana, I wouldn't have gotten the help I needed. Furthermore, I also believe that God's mighty hand was guiding me to the right time and place for me to change. That would ultimately be in hancock County!

So God prevented me from getting arrested in Louisiana. I believe that is divine intervention at its best. The real reason why the Slidell, Louisiana cop handed me off is that God's mighty hand guided me right into the arms of the only people in all of humanity, who would help inspire me to change my life and not just me, but countless others. I owe my life to the people of the great city of Bay St. Louis, Mississippi. I believe there was no other place on Earth for me to get the miracle of salvation and transformation. There is no doubt in my mind that the good Lord's timing is impeccable! I also believe wholeheartedly all of the Lord of Lords and King of King's horses and men were perfectly lined up in Hancock County to get me to my eternal destiny. I have seen so many people die since I have been here in Hancock County of drug overdoses. I'm so grateful to be alive.

Then another strange coincidence occurred. The real reason I stopped at the second exit off Interstate 10, at a motel that I normally wouldn't stay at if it were the last one on earth, because of how it looked. Coincidentally, I was at the hotel exactly the same time a Hancock County Deputy was driving by with a tag reader on his vehicle in the parking lot of the motel I was at. Wow, I tell you what, I either have the worst luck on earth, not that I believe in luck, but my point is, there seems to be a pattern here! But I do believe in divine intervention. I believe I had a divine appointment to step into my God-given destiny that fateful October night. There is definitely another unseen force working in my favor here, guiding me into the perfect position to get the help I needed. Getting me poised for the miracle that a preacher from Texas told me I was poised for, which I so desperately needed and wanted. Most importantly, I had been praying about it for seventeen long years.

If I had kept going a few more exits, I would have been in a different county. Coincidentally, I had planned to drive at least one more hour east that night. If I had kept driving to a different county. I wouldn't have got the help that I so desperately needed, and I would have forever remained hopeless in active addiction, surrendering my life to the disease of addiction and no doubt I would die in my sin. The truth is that fentanyl runs rampant in this part of the country. I wholeheartedly believe that God knew I had to be removed from society and incarcerated right then and there to save me from imminent death.

Then one day, while I'm at the door of the pod I'm housed in, waiting to go to an Alcoholics Anonymous meeting inside the Hancock County Jail. I committed a random act of kindness after being prompted by the Holy Spirit and I let someone go ahead of me. As it turns out, that would be the catalyst that would spark a lifelong friendship between my mentor Dan Munger and me. I'm sure Dan has seen at least one hundred thousand random acts of kindness at seventy years old. Why did Dan see that random act of kindness? I will tell you why, because Almighty God inspired it. Dan Munger has the mind of Christ. Dan sees spiritual things and listens with his spiritual ears. Is that not a coincidence? God knew that Dan was the man on this side of Heaven to get me to my eternal destination.

I also believe that God used Dan Munger to put favor in the heart of the Warden for me. If it wasn't for Dan Munger speaking those positive faith-filled words to the Warden about me being an "honest man." There is no doubt in my mind that many things wouldn't have happened for me in Hancock County and I would be sitting in a prison somewhere in Mississippi right now, wasting away. Also to say the least, this book never happens. The treatment center I'm starting definitely doesn't occur and I sure don't become a Psychology major at America's largest Christian university.

Another coincidence was when I spoke at the Chainbreaker's graduation in front of Sheriff Ricky Adam, Warden Brandon

Zeringue, Judge Hoda, and all the inmates' families. Then the old man afterward came up to me and said, "I think you just found your calling." God had prompted that man to say that to me. That was God's way of affirming that I was on the right track and should hold my course at all costs. If you really think about it, ould that coincidence be the Lord prompting me to stay at the Hancock County Jail because he had a ministry for me here? When I spoke that day, it helped me be known because I wasn't from Hancock County. This would help me become known to the Hancock County Administration So I could later become an inmate worker. The reason why is very simple. If I don't become an inmate worker, nothing happens for me in Hancock County.

Then the biggest coincidence in the history of the human race occurs! All these people would end up at exactly the same place, at the same time, and I would end up in a jail exactly where they all were, and have every last one of them show me compassion and favor that God put in their hearts toward me, even when some of them didn't believe in God or me. This would happen in a foreign town where I was a total stranger. Coincidentally, on top of all that. I would be willing to change at the exact time and place. Wow, hold on my friend! You just read this book. I wasn't willing to change; I was willing to think about it if my circumstances were bad enough.

I was arrested twenty-four times in multiple states. But the good Lord made my heart willing to change in Hancock County. All of these things happening the way they did without divine intervention is as impossible as me trying to make all the stars align, in a single file line, across the sky on my own accord. There is no way all these coincidences are happenstance and circumstance. That many coincidences in the same zip code, much less the same place, can only be orchestrated by the Most High God.

Wow! There is nothing that is impossible with God! God is great and He made a believer out of me! The Heavenly Hosts were working overtime and sometimes angels are just genuinely good human beings helping their fellow man. But make no mistake, God is in them, acting according to his will and good pleasure. Like those good folks at the Hancock County Sheriff's Office. I sincerely believe that all this happened because it was divine intervention to get me to my God-given destiny, which is greatness. Most importantly, it has also allowed God to help countless people through me and all to his glory. Just like now, Almighty God is trying to inspire you through me. He is doing this to get you to your God-given destiny. What about the coincidence of me taking five years instead of three years because I had a ministry here at the jail? Even though everything in me said, "Go home to your family; you have got kids."

But deep down inside, I knew God wanted me to stay here at the Hancock County Jail. I knew and believed the good Lord had a plan. I decided to stay in faith and then in the thirty-ninth month of my incarceration, just right past the point of three years, here at the Hancock County Jail. The good Lord blessed me because of my obedience and inspired me to write this book to help others. Then completely unknown to me at the time, it was all to give my heart back. God gave me a new heart. A heart with just as much compassion for people as my friends at the Hancock County Sheriff's Office. I poured my heart out to help my fellow man in this book. I did it all to God's glory in the hope of inspiring people like you to be all you can be in the Army of God. Coincidentally, a man reaps what he sows. I try to help people get their hearts right with the Lord and it keeps mine right. Imagine that the law of reaping and sowing is true. What a coincidence, the law of reaping and sowing is in the Bible, the gospel truth. My point is that there is no way on God's green earth that this is anything but divine intervention. I believe it is all a part of God's plan to get me to my eternal destiny and more importantly, to get you to your rightful place in eternity.

Today I sincerely hope that Almighty God has inspired you to follow Jesus Christ and trust him as your Lord and Savior. Like the good Lord did for me on that fateful October night in South Mississippi. I sincerely hope that you can see God's mighty hand working for you, in your life, for your eternal good. I believe you will and I hope you give God the glory in every area of your life. God is worthy of the glory in your life and all of creation. God bless you my friend and I hope you never forget that God loves you. I also hope you never forget that God can do what you can't do for yourself, and nothing is impossible with God!

Upon completion of this book, I viewed my arrest records. I was completely accurate with the timeline. I was arrested twenty-four times in multiple states. As of right now on October 23, 2022, I'm still wanted by multiple agencies in Texas. When I get to that day of reckoning with my past in Texas. There is no doubt that God will do what the Bible says, "He will make my righteousness shine like the dawn and the justice for my cause like the noonday sun" (Psalm 37:6). I know and believe that I will not die in prison. I believe what the Bible says, "The number of my days God will fulfill" (Exodus 23:26). I also believe that God will bring my family back together and "As for me and my house, we will serve the Lord'" (Joshua 24:15). God is an awesome God! I am living proof that God is true to his word. The Bible says, "Then, even if your beginnings were modest, your final days will be full of prosperity" (Job 8:7). Since I have been walking with the Lord, I have been tremendously blessed. I have never wanted for anything. I also know that when I stand in front of the judge in three counties back in Texas. That for the first time in my entire life. I will have a clear conscience before God and my fellow man. Most importantly, I know that only God can judge me and when I stand before Almighty God in the highest court in all of creation. I will have a clear conscience before God. I know that because my redeemer Jesus Christ lives. That is what truly matters in this life. That is the difference maker in my life today. The God factor! There is no doubt that I will by God's grace and my faith in the Lord Jesus Christ, be judged not guilty. After surviving all I just went through, I have come to one startling realization: I am literally a living, breathing, walking, modern-day miracle and I'm free at last.

The purpose of my telling you all this is to bring you to a place where you can see how Christ has saved and transformed your life. Over the last four years, I have had the privilege of witnessing to thousands of people about the goodness of God. I have spoken at multiple churches, treatment centers, and schools and teach a rehab and two theology courses. I did it all for Jesus, by the grace of God. I'm so thankful to God for giving me true life in Jesus Christ. I have seen a lot of people convert to Christianity in my lifetime. I want to talk to you about something very near and dear to my heart. I made a profession of faith when I was twelve years old. I told you that.

What is so amazing to me as I look back now is that I really truly believed I was saved. The process of conversion can be compared to vaccination. "Oh, I did that, we say." What is even crazier to me as I look back now is that I really believed I was a Christian, as I was doing everything you just read. I said, the so-called "sinner's prayer." That meant I was saved, right? That meant I could say or do anything I wanted to and nothing could pluck me out of the hands of God, right? I was told that God loves us all unconditionally and that once I was saved, I was always saved! The truth is that if you are saved, you are always saved!

I really believed in my heart that I could say, think, or do anything I wanted to and not live by the narrow way of the Bible and still be saved. That thought process is just as insane as my former life that you just read about in this book. I believed what I'm telling you for twenty-nine years as I walked on people like a doormat and tried to have God serve me instead of me serving him. In other words, I was the god of my world. I know this now because as I look back on my actions in my former life. I realize now that although I said, "I believe in you, Lord," with my lips. I never, not for one second of my former life, loved God in truth and action, as the Bible talks about. All the while, I truly believed that I was a Christian. My style of life didn't ever point to me surrendering to the measure and stature of Jesus Christ. I realize now that I was greatly deceived and I'm pitiful without Jesus Christ for a single second!

The really crazy thing is that I surrendered to chaos in my former life instead of surrendering to Christ. As I truly believed myself to be a Christian in my former life. If you ask anyone who ever had an encounter with me in my former way of life, when I was on that "broad road" that Jesus talked about in the Bible that leads to destruction, there is no doubt in my mind that not one person would acknowledge that I was a Christian or ever acted like I was in my former life. My point is that I believed I was a Christian and a child of God because I said the "sinner's prayer." You just read this book. That is absolutely preposterous! There wasn't a true repentance when I said the sinner's prayer or what some would say about the sinner's prayer, and call it a baseless "cataract of nonsense."

Let me show you what the Bible teaches about salvation. In the next few pages, as I finish this book. I have got to warn you. I'm about to say things that might make you very angry. But I say these things clothed in Christlike humility. I have studied God's word intently for forty-nine months like my eternity depends on it. But more importantly, like someone's eternity depends on it through me. I am not talking about reading the Bible leisurely. There is a huge difference and when you study the Bible intently, there is a blessing that comes from it. That blessing comes from God by way of the Holy Spirit. It is divine revelation and inspiration. I didn't first notice what I'm about to unleash upon you. But as I was sitting in the Chaplain's office editing this book one morning. I prayed to God like I had so many other mornings before I started editing his book and said, "Father, is there something I have missed in your book? Please show me what to do, Father. Why on earth is this taking so long?" Then suddenly it felt like someone had just walked into the room with me. The hair on the back of my neck stood straight up. I went to get a reference from the Bible on a popular website and this message hit me like a ton of bricks. I received divine revelation of a magnitude that is unfathomable. This is what I learned in seventeen minutes.

## THE TRUE, FORGOTTEN MESSAGE OF THE GOSPEL AND CHRISTIANITY

*"I'm about to preach to you like a dying man. To dying men, women, and children. I'm about to tell you some things that you might misunderstand. But if I correctly interpret this passage of scriptures I'm going to give you, it will be as though God were*

speaking through a man, and your problem will not be with me. It will be with God and his word. So the only question to be decided here is whether I am a false prophet. Or am I telling you the truth? If I'm telling you the truth, then nothing else matters. But conforming your life to that truth. My dear friend, if I am a false prophet. I should be terrified because I stand condemned before the Most High God. If I am telling you the truth, you should be horribly afraid when you stand before God if you get this wrong. I beg of you to listen to me very closely. Like all of your eternity depends on it.

This is the true Gospel of Jesus Christ. Matthew 7:13-23 says, "Enter by the narrow gate. For the gate is wide, and the way is easy that leads to destruction, and those who enter by it are many. (14) "For the gate is narrow, and the way is hard that leads to life, and those who find it are few. (15) "Beware of the false prophets, who come to you in sheep's clothing but inwardly are ravenous wolves. (16) "You will recognize them by their fruits. Are grapes gathered from thornbushes or figs from thistles? (17) "So, every healthy tree bears good fruit, but the diseased tree bears bad fruit. (18) "A healthy tree cannot bear bad fruit, nor can a diseased tree bear good fruit. (19) "Every tree that does not bear good fruit is cut down and thrown into the fire. (20) "Thus you will recognize them by their fruits. (21) "Not everyone who says to me, 'Lord, Lord,' will enter into the kingdom of heaven, but the one who does the will of my Father who is in heaven. (22) "On that day many will say to me, 'Lord, Lord,' did we not prophesy in your name and cast out demons in your name, and do mighty works in your name?' (23) "And then I will declare to them, 'I never knew you; depart from me, you workers of lawlessness (Matthew 7:13-23, ESV).

As I sit here today, I want you to know that I have been to the depths of the grave trying to find my way in life. I'm not troubled *in my heart. I'm not concerned with your self-esteem or your goals. I'm not concerned with the terrible things that are going on in the world today. There is only one thing that has really truly troubled me for the last forty-five months. That one thing is that the vast majority of people here on earth could possibly be in Hell in the next seventy-five years. Sadly, many who even profess Jesus Christ as Lord will spend an eternity in Hell. WHAT YOU NEED TO KNOW IS THAT SALVATION IS BY FAITH AND FAITH ALONE IN JESUS CHRIST. Faith alone in Jesus Christ is preceded and followed by repentance. A turning away from sin. A hatred for the things God hates and a love for the things that God loves. A growing in holiness and a desire not to be like your worldly heroes, not to be like the world, and not to be like the great majority of Christians, BUT TO BE LIKE JESUS CHRIST!*

*I didn't write this book to get recognition, money, fame, and fortune. I wrote this book because I love the Lord and you. More importantly, God wants you to know the truth about the narrow road that few are on. Also, you should believe wholeheartedly that God loves you. You know what the Bible tells Christians to do? Examine yourself, and test yourself in light of scripture so that you can see if you are in the faith.*

*The Bible says, that even our greatest works are like filthy rags before God, and because of that, you know what we deserve. We deserve the wrath of God. The holy hatred of God. One might say, "Wait a minute. God doesn't hate anybody. God is Love." No, my friend, you need to understand something. Jesus Christ, the prophets, and the Apostles taught this. That apart from the grace of God revealed in Jesus Christ our Lord. That the only thing left for you is the wrath and fierce anger of God. This is because of your rebellion and sin against God. I hear people say all the time that God can't hate because God is Love. I tell you that God must hate because God is love. You see, I love*

220

children. Therefore I hate abortion. If I love that which is holy, I must hate that which is unholy. God is a holy God, which is something the vast majority of Christians in modern society have forgotten about.

Listen to me. If you're saved, do you know why you're saved? You're not saved because the Romans and Jews rejected Jesus. You're not saved because they put a crown of thorns on his head. You're not saved because they ran a spear through his side. You're not saved because they nailed him to the cross. Do you know why you are saved if you're saved? It is because when Jesus Christ was hanging on that cross. He bore your sins. The sin of God's people and all the fierce wrath of God that should have fallen upon you. Fell upon God's only begotten son.

People say the cross is a sign of how much man is worth. That is not true! The cross is a sign of how depraved we really are! That it took the death of God's own son. It was the only thing that could save people like us. The death of God's own son under the wrath of his own Father. Jesus Christ being resurrected was powerful. It was God's way of saying, "This is the gospel of Jesus."

Conversion is not like a flu shot. Oh, I did that, I repented, and I believed. The question is, my friend. Are you continuing to repent and believe? The Bible says, "He who began a good work in you will finish it." The Bible never teaches that a person can be a genuine Christian and live in continuous carnality, wickedness, and sin all the days of their life. But the Bible teaches that the genuine Christian has been given a new nature. The genuine Christian has a Father who loves, disciplines, and cares for them. In the Bible, Jesus indicates that one of the principal signs of being a genuine Christian is that you will walk in the narrow way.

*I'm not saying that a Christian is without sin. But what I'm getting at is this. If you are genuinely a born-again Christian—a child of God—you will walk in the way of righteousness as a style of life. Then when you step off that narrow path. The Father will come for you. He will discipline you and put you back on the path of righteousness. But if you profess to have gone through the narrow gate and live in the broad way just like all the unbelievers in the world. The Bible wants you to know that you should be terribly, terribly afraid!*

*We have forgotten to believe that salvation is a supernatural work of God, and those who have generally been converted, and regenerated by the power of the Holy Spirit, are going to be a new creature. The Bible says, "That if any man be in Christ. He is a new creature." The Bible says, "Beware of the false prophets, who come to you in sheep's clothing, but inwardly are ravenous wolves." One of the greatest distinguishing marks of a false prophet is that he will always tell you what you want to hear. He will never rain on your parade; he will keep you clapping, jumping, dizzy, and entertained. He will also present a Christianity to you that makes your church look like a three-ringed circus and a Six Flags over Jesus.*

*You will know them by their fruits. How do you truly know that you're saved? Was it because someone told you, you prayed a prayer, or because you believed? How do you know you believe? Everyone says they believe. How do you know you're not like that? The Bible says, "even the demons believe and shudder at the fact" in the book of James. Do you know how the Bible teaches that you know you are saved? You know that you are saved because your life is in the process of being changed, and your style of life is one of walking in the paths of God's truth. Then when you step off those paths in disobedience, as we all do. The good Lord comes for you and puts you back on the path.*

What is the fruit that you are bearing? Do you look like the world? Do you act like the world? Can you have and experience the same joys that the world experiences? Do you love sin and relish it? Do you love rebellion and relish it? Then you probably don't know God.

Let me take it a step further. Let's say I was to speak at a church at ten o'clock on Sunday morning. The meeting is over at eleven. It just so happens that I don't get there until ten fifty-five. When I walk in, the pastor looks at me and says, "Brother O'Dell, you're late. Don't you appreciate the fact that you have an opportunity to speak here this morning?" I then turn around and say, "Yes, but you have to forgive me, brother. I was out on the highway. I had a flat tire. I changed the tire and put the lug nuts back on. Suddenly, one rolled out in the middle of the highway. I rushed out to get it and picked it up. I heard something and looked up, and there was a thirty-ton diesel truck coming right at me at about a hundred miles per hour. Then it hit me, and that is why I am late." The pastor would look at me and say, "Brother O'Dell, that's absurd! It is impossible for you to have an encounter with a thirty ton diesel truck and not be changed." Now my question is to you, my dear friend. What is larger? A thirty ton diesel truck or God? How is it that so many people today have had an encounter with Jesus Christ, and yet they are not permanently changed?

The Bible says, anyone who does not bear good fruit is cut down and thrown into the fire. What was Jesus talking about? My dear friend, he was talking about the judgment of Almighty God that will fall upon you, me, and the world. Matthew 7:21 says, "Not everyone who says to me, 'Lord, Lord,' will enter the kingdom of heaven, but the one who does the will of my Father." This fellow, in verse twenty-one, isn't someone who just suddenly decided it's judgment day, and I better profess Jesus as Lord. This is a person who emphatically declares to other people that Jesus Christ is Lord. He walks around saying, "Lord." He dances in front of the musicians, saying, "Lord." He sings the songs of the Lord. But Jesus says to him, "Depart from me. I never knew you". There are many people that are going to profess 'Lord, Lord'. My dear precious brother or sister. Are you one of them?

Matthew 7:21 says, "If you want to go to heaven, you must do the will of the Father." What happened to the truth? The truth tells you this. The evidence, the way that you can have assurance that you are genuinely a born-again Christian, is that you do, as a style of life, the will of the Father! I AM NOT TALKING ABOUT WORKS. I'm talking about evidence of faith. How do you know the faith that you have is not false? This is how you know. You practice a style of life concerned with doing the will of the Father, and if you practice the will of the Father, when you disobey the will of the Father, the Holy Spirit comes and convicts you, and God puts you back on the narrow path again. If you can play around in sin. If you can love the world and the things of this world. Oh, my dear friend, listen to my voice! There's a good chance you do not know God and do not belong to him.

Matthew 7:23 says, "And then I will declare to them, 'I never knew you; depart from me." People say, "The most important thing on Earth is to know Jesus Christ." That is not true! The most important thing on earth is that Jesus Christ knows you. Let me put it this way. If I walk up to the White House tomorrow. I promise the Secret Service will not let me in if I say, "I know the President." But if the President walks out and says, "He knows me." They will let me in. It is the same way with Jesus Christ and Heaven. You can profess to know Jesus Christ. But my question to you is, does Jesus know you?

*There are two ways. A narrow way and a broad way. Which one are you on? There are two types of trees. A good tree that bears good fruit and is going to Heaven. A bad tree that bears bad fruit and will be cut down and thrown into the fires of Hell. There are those who profess Jesus as Lord and do the will of the Father in Heaven, and there are those who profess Jesus as Lord and do not do the will of the Father in Heaven, and they go to Hell. This is not because of a lack of works. It is because of a lack of faith demonstrated. Faith without works is dead faith.*

*Let's get down to doctrine. What does the word of God say? How does your life stand in front of that blazing fire which is the holiness of God? ON THAT FINAL DAY, WILL YOUR CONFESSION HOLD TRUE? You need to know. How you know is by going into the word of God and obeying it. You must bring every thought, deed, and word into the subjection of Jesus Christ. (SHOCKING Sermon | Paul Washer | Inspirational & Motivational Video, 2020).*

*Let me ask you a question. When was the last time you wept over your sin? When was the last time you were broken over your sin? You have not sinned against an inferior prince. You have not sinned against the President of the United States. You have not sinned against your fellow man. YOU HAVE SINNED AGAINST THE LORD OF GLORY. The Lord of Lords and the King of Kings. Look at the horrid wretchedness of sin, the vulgarity, the prostitution of sin. It is a horrid thing. It is a beast waiting at the door, and its desire is to have you. The Bible says, "For the wages of sin is death; but the gift of God is eternal life through Jesus Christ our Lord" (Romans 6:23, KJV).*

I want you to listen to me. I want for you what I almost died searching for, which is for you to receive the love of Almighty God in Christ Jesus. All that will matter on that final day is one thing. Did your life honor Jesus Christ to the glory of God, or did you waste it on yourself? I realize as I look back now that as I laid in the holding cell that day, in booking, at the Hancock County Jail, one of the main reasons I was able to get healing and change is very simple: I lost all hope in self-righteousness. In retrospect, I needed to lose all hope in myself. To be able to find the true Hope in Jesus Christ that turned the world upside down. When I lost all hope in myself, I was poised for my greatest miracle, and I was able to find the Living Hope and it was all through Jesus Christ, my Lord.

Jesus Christ healed me of one of my greatest maladies—fear. Fear is the opposite of faith. Fear had crippled me physically and spiritually my whole life. When I was healed of my fear, I realized my greatest asset was faith, and I could walk by faith in the Lord Jesus Christ. I was healed by the grace of God, and my faith demonstrated toward God through Jesus Christ. I was like the man in the Bible at Soloman's Colonnade, healed after thirty-nine years through his faith demonstrated. I am so happy Jesus knows me. I'm grateful to be healed and transformed. I Thank God every day that I'm able to live by faith. The Bible says, "The righteous will live by faith." I thank God that I am the righteousness of God in Christ Jesus and that I can and will do all things through Christ who strengthens me. God bless you, and may the grace of the Lord be with you.